UNPLUGGED

A JOURNEY OF THE MIND, SOUL, AND STRENGTH

"BE NOT CONFORMED TO THIS WORLD
BUT BE YE TRANSFORMED,
BY THE RENEWING OF YOUR MIND."

THOMAS L. TEAL JR

ACKNOWLEDGMENT

First and foremost, I would like to thank the Lord Jesus Christ, to whom I am eternally indebted for the blood He shed for the redemption of my soul. This book is my way of giving back to Him and to others with the hope of changing lives. His Word and His Spirit have eternally changed my life forever. I thank you, Lord Jesus.

To my Pastor, W.J. Davidson, indeed, a man sent from God: Pastor, your forty-plus years of laboring in the gospel to prepare a people for the Lord has been an unwavering example of dedication and a continual inspiration. Without your teaching, this book would never be possible; thank you, sir.

To my wife, Laura Teal, the epitome of what a woman of God is. Laura, you are the definition of what Proverbs 31 defines as a virtuous woman. You have been an anchor to our family and me. I love you and thank you for the inspiration to push me to write this book. It could never have happened without you looking at me one night before going to bed and saying to me, *"You need to write a book called "Unplugged."*

To my children Samantha, Faith, Boaz, my son-in-law Judah, and my daughter-in-law and my granddaughter Priscilla: Outside of Jesus Christ, no one else has impacted or changed my life more than you. You are the best; your love for God and His truth radiates in and out of your life. Thank you all for your dedication to the Lord.

To my parents, Thomas Teal Sr. and Carol Sawgle. Without you, none of this would have been possible. Thank you for choosing life; unlike so many others who find themselves in your shoes as teenagers, you accepted the difficult one instead of taking the easy route, for my sake. I love you both for your courage and sacrifice.

Sadly, Dad, you passed before this was ever finalized or published. I can remember talking to you on the phone the next day after deciding to write it. You were worried about Eve (Erika) getting upset because she was also a writer, and you expressed your concerns about us being competitive (he knew us well). However, I want the world to read and know that you were an incredible influence in my life and the best dad. Even when I didn't show it, nor did it reflect in my actions at times, your words of wisdom were in my head, trying to guide me. There will never be a man like you. Every morning when I sit in front of my computer to write, your pictures and the moments we shared look back at me, reminding me how precious life is and how it can be taken away in the blink of an eye. You are missed dearly.

To my oldest sister Erika: Thank you so much for your constant support and our daily talks on the phone about writers' stuff. What an inspiration you are to me. You are an incredible writer, and your passion for it manifests in who you are. Your footprints are all throughout this book. The patience and long-suffering you had during the miserable editing of this manuscript with all its mistakes are to be highly commended! This indeed wouldn't have been possible without you. You are a Rockstar!

To my sister Ivonne: Your life is an incredible book in itself. You faced death on multiple occasions, overcame impossible odds, and never accepted any other option but victory. You are an amazing person and an awesome sister.

To my youngest sister Ashley: You helped edit this in its infant stage – the horrible rough draft, and when I say rough, I mean rough! Thank you for all your help; I love you.

To my stepmother Julie: You are a reader's reader, and I don't think I've ever seen you without a book, nor do I ever recall you or dad fighting in over thirty years of marriage to dad. I'm sure you guys did, but I never saw you disrespect him or argue with him, and I want you to know what an excellent example of a wife you are.

To my other little sister April May Sawgle: we have had our moments growing up, both good and bad; I want the best life has for you, and I pray that this book might help you in that process.

To James Bommer, my friend for life and brother in the Lord: Thank you for your honesty and the sacrifice in taking the time to edit my manuscript. Also, one of our many adventures from our childhood is illustrated in this book. God has brought us a mighty long way.

The most remarkable advice I have been given as an aspiring author was from Zari, the first editor to look at my manuscript. This may be common knowledge in the writing world, but never having a writing class or being involved in this arena was brilliant to me. Zari's advice to me was to write a paragraph about each chapter's title describing what each chapter is about. If the chapter's content doesn't align with the description, delete it or save it for another place in the book. That tidbit of wisdom changed the entire course of this book. Thanks, Zari, for sharing your knowledge.

To Lillian Bommer (Jim's daughter): Lilly, you are one amazing young lady who has been imbued with an incredible gift of writing and editing. I'm praying God blesses whatever you decide to do in the writer's world because what you possess needs to be shared with this world. You were the icing on the cake, and by no means could this book have turned out the way it did without you.

David Green, a.k.a "Hemingway": I could write a book on how much you've impacted my life and helped make this dream become a reality. Thank you for our writers' thread, the daily words of encouragement, sharing your thoughts, and for all the time you spent one summer editing this book. Thank you for your brutal honesty and for enduring my lackluster writing skills. You are a fantastic writer, teacher, preacher, and friend. Thank you, David; I could not have done it without you as well.

Rachel Green (David's wife): Thank you for taking the time to read this and coming up with the brilliant idea of incorporating portions of the book into the journal.

Emily Lisa from Fiverr a.k.a. writeralways16: You put the finishing touches on it and polished it up for print, great job.

Akira007 from Fiverr, thank you for your longsuffering during the designing of the cover, and an excellent job.

I want to thank you, the reader who purchases this book. This journey is one that we'll have taken together, obviously at different points and on different paths, nevertheless, still the same forty days of being *"unplugged."*

I'm looking forward to hearing about your journey. *(thomaslteal@ gmail.com)* My prayer is that you will find the answers to your questions on your journey. The sole purpose of this book is to help others the way it helped me.

Unplugged was birthed out of a desire for a closer walk with the Lord and clarity in understanding His Will for my life. My prayer is that God blesses you and directs you on your path to His Will for your life.

PROLOGUE

Like the old saying goes, *"I'm sick and tired of being sick and tired."* It's the moment in life when change can no longer be delayed or avoided, and the rubber has met the road. I'm not just talking about change, but a radical shift in apoplectic proportion, the kind of change that makes people around you question your sanity. That's how my journey began. Life has a way of slowly tangling you up in its web ever so subtly --before you know it, its tentacles have wrapped themselves around you, squeezing the life out of you. This doesn't happen overnight. The process is gradual and unhurried, morphed into what we have come to know as *"the way life goes."*

Accepting things as they are without ever going against the grain means you have surrendered to living life according to the *"status quo"* and going through the motions. Let me tell you that you are better than the *"status quo"* life, and you deserve so much better. Yes, really! You have much more potential; in fact, this book and with the Lord's help will help you achieve it.

The Lord made a statement that opens a door that allows you to go from the status quo life into a life that exceeds all your hopes and aspirations. He said, ***"I have come that you might have life, and you might have it more abundantly"*** (John 10:10). An abundant life is not a *status quo life;* it is a life filled with endless opportunities. This book has many opportunities that will help lead you to the *"abundant life."* Every page is a door, and they are waiting for you to walk through. All you have to do is turn the page, and another opportunity for *abundant life* will present itself. That's where I was at, stuck in the rut of life, and I wanted a change and to have a closer walk with the Lord and a more *abundant life* with Him. Some people search for the answers on how to solve the mysterious puzzle of getting out of the box, while others remain enslaved, unable to escape the trap of being *"sick and tired of being sick and tired."* You are not that person because you picked this book up and decided that you would break the mold your life has formed into while others remain trapped in. Woefully, they adhere to this way of thinking and accepting it as it's just the way life goes, and these are the cards I've been dealt in life. Yes, life can be unfair, and it may seem like the deck is stacked against you, but with God, all things are possible! The mindset of the defeated is unable to break the chains that shackle them in the mundane. They become numb to anything that might resemble freedom. Why? Because "change" is a fearful thing; therefore, they are resolved to accept the status quo as life!

That's not you. You are not resolved to accept the mundane as abundant life. If you want better for yourself, your family, and your friends, it starts with you. It starts with *"unplugging!"* There is an old phrase wrestlers refer to in training, and it's very applicable to what unplugging is about; it's called *"embrace the grind."* Get ready to grind! This book will lead you to some areas in your life that will become uncomfortable; that is where you'll have to embrace the grind to get through it. The definition of insanity is doing the same thing repeatedly and expecting different results; unplugging will make those results different.

A song written in the '70s by the band Aerosmith sums it up best: *"The Same Old Song And Dance."* The song is about going through the motions of life without ever-changing. I heard this song growing up throughout the years but never fully understood it until I found my life had become *"The Same Old Song and Dance!"* Music was a big part of my life (and in my family). Ever since the age of seven, I have wanted to be a rock star. My grandfather and my father both played electric guitar, so by default, I followed suit, with the dreams and aspirations of not only playing guitar but making my living doing it. I would put on my parent's albums and their 45's, and, on occasion, an eight-track (I'm really dating myself) and play air guitar, imagining I was playing those songs. I loved music.

I joined America's workforce at age sixteen, working in the produce fields of Imlay City, MI. I worked and saved until I had enough money to buy my first electric guitar from a friend of mine. It was a blue Magnum Fender Strat knockoff. It wasn't much, but it was the starting point of my dreams. This guitar would soon become the breeding ground for honing my craft and the foundation for building my skills. By the time I was twenty, I was playing in a real band. The band started out covering songs that were popular with our circle of friends and on the radio. However, it wasn't long before we started writing original songs and playing in clubs. We were a thrash metal band, loud, fast, aggressive music with heavily distorted guitars. I had finally found a remedy for my inner illness.

Music was a channel to release all my aggression; it was my passion, and playing loud and fast was my cure. However, the music by the mid-'90s scene had taken on a strange platform. A new trend had crept into the music scene, and many bands were testing the waters. It was labeled *"unplugged."* It was an entirely acoustic gig. Bands of all genres were starting to play their music in this non-electrified state. There were no loud Marshall Amplifiers piercing your eardrums as they pushed the envelope on the decimal chart. There were no blistering guitar solos laced with distortion, no wah-wah pedals, nothing. It was just undefiled raw guitar, pure and natural.

The word unplugged was first used in 1990, and it refers to a musical performance without electrical instruments or amplifiers. In my own words, I would say it was a natural performance, unmodified, undisturbed, and untainted by technology. In like fashion, over the next forty days, you will become unmodified, undisturbed, and untainted by technology or whatever your life is plugged into. It's not going to be easy, but it's your goal. Are you up for the challenge? I believe you are because you're *"sick and tired of being sick and tired."* Your determination to overcome the mundane will catapult you to be victorious in this challenge.

One day after doing some self-evaluation in my spiritual walk, I decided I would become *"unplugged."* I told my family that I was *"unplugging"* for a while because I wanted to see God do a miracle for us! No Facebook, no YouTube, no videos of any sort, just general and local news. Later that night, as we were getting ready for bed, I told Laura what I was doing and why. She looked at me and said, *"You need to write a book called 'Unplugged.'"* I really can't explain what happened to me when she said that, but all I can say is that it struck a chord that resonated with me. When I woke up the next morning, I told myself that I would do it and so began the process of writing this book.

This started as a challenge to be *"unplugged"* from all the media that our lives are hard-wired into, such as Facebook, Instagram, Twitter, YouTube, television, or whatever else that may consume the majority of your free time. Then I realized this might not be feasible for everyone, especially if your job requires you to be involved in social media. However, there are other things you are *"plugged"* into that you can *"unplug"* from and work on your abundant life. This book started out *"unplugging"* oneself from the influence of media, technology, or devices; I soon realized that there is a whole lot more that you need to become *"unplugged"* from.

There are hurts you need to unplug. Things in your past, resentment, and most importantly, whatever is fueling those inner demons that torment you. After contemplating this, I wondered what kind of statement would it make to those that follow you on Twitter, Instagram, and Facebook if you made a post stating that you are *'unplugging yourself for the next forty days?'*

For the next forty days, you are going to bombard your mind with spiritual influences. You will commit to daily reading, not daily tweeting or posting. You will begin your forty days of spiritual saturation, reading, and prayer. I'll tell you what will happen to me after I did this challenge. You will reinvigorate your walk with the Lord, the people around you, and your mind and your thoughts won't be clouded. Forty days of *plugging* into nothing but spiritual resources will jumpstart your life back into a higher spiritual place in God.

What kind of impact do you think *unplugging* would have on your friends and family if they took this challenge because of the change they have seen in you? If you look back in history at any great revival, it began with people getting serious about their walk with God. How do you think it would affect your congregations and your attendance to your church services if you *unplugged* from the things of the world and *plugged* more into the Word of God? My personal experience was unbelievable and life-changing. Spiritual doors have opened that I don't believe could have ever opened if it wasn't for this challenge. Do you want a change? Do you want doors to open? Do you want a personal revival to happen in your life? I believe the answer is yes, to all the above. Let's embark on this challenge together, so an opportunity can present itself. Get ready to *unplug*.

Initially, when I sat down to write this book, I had no forethought, plot, outline, and, to be honest, no real sense of direction. All I knew was I had to go on this journey, and I strongly felt the calling of God to write *unplugged*. The basis for this book was purely inspirational. I draw a large portion of the narrative is from the life of Joseph. Why Joseph? Primarily outside of the Lord himself and Job, not many others had to conquer their inner demons by *unplugging* as Joseph did. One of the most amazing things about Joseph's life is the relatability to ours. Through many trials and tribulations, Joseph's encounters in life seem to run parallel and harmonious with the lives of so many people you see today. Like Joseph, Job, and the Lord, you can have a victorious finish if you are willing to face the task at hand. Letting go and letting God begins with *unplugging*. If you've never read Joseph's story, do yourself a favor and read Genesis chapters 37-60.

TABLE OF CONTENTS

CHAPTER 1

IT'S TIME TO CUT THE CORD AND BECOME "UNPLUGGED"

The first step of cutting the cord is to realize that you are *plugged* into something. Only you know whatever it is that robs you of your spiritual time with the Lord. Perhaps you're *"plugged"* into an emotion that has been haunting you from your past or a bad relationship. Maybe, you're plugged into things, and you don't even realize it? I can assure you, taking this challenge will open up your eyes in many areas of your life. Cutting the cord will not be easy, but it will be well worth it.

I believe that after completing this forty-day challenge of no media, or whatever else it is you're challenging, your outlook, perspective, and relationship with others will change for the better. It's becoming more and more evident that this entire world is entangled in the "worldwide web." Almost everything you associate with is tied directly to it. Society has become woven into it, like fabric in a garment, and there is no escaping it unless you become entirely unplugged and go off the grid. Sadly, most have become so dependent on it that they can't even function without it.

There has never been a generation like today. People are exposed to more information than ever before. If you Google a simple question, hundreds if not thousands of web pages appear. The internet generation is unlike any other culture we've ever seen. Children are seeing and hearing far too prematurely in life.

There are web pages filled with pornographic content, violence, human trafficking, and every ungodly thing you can imagine. Everyone has become an internet expert simply by clicking; you have all your answers. Even the most ridiculous of all voices demand to be taken with seriousness, and if you disagree, you are dismissed as being undemocratic elitism. It's called the "dumbing down of expertise." People put more trust in a web page than in an individual that has spent ten to twelve years in college and has thirty years of on-the-job experience.

The reality is that there is no way you can escape it. However, that doesn't mean it has to control. *Unplugging* is about taking control of areas of your life that are out of control. As a 47-year-old man, I come from a generation where there was no Internet or smartphones. We didn't have Facebook, Instagram, or all the other social media platforms out there today. Growing up, there wasn't an overwhelming onslaught of media waves bombarding our minds daily. This type of assault has had a crippling effect on society.

IF YOU WANT TO HAVE CHANGE, IT BEGINS WITH YOU

With an ever-changing world that is always on the move, it is effortless to get caught up in the melee of life and the social pressures that burden you. You become lost and don't even realize it until you push the pause button.

"Sometimes, you have to step back to see the trees from the forest."

This book's premise is that sometimes you have to step back and see precisely what is moving, changing, and going on in your life and adjust accordingly.

IT'S TIME TO UNPLUG FROM THE MAYHEM

Philippians 2:5 says, *"Let this mind be in you, which was also in Christ Jesus,"* the mindset is where the battle begins.

Everything begins with your mindset/thoughts. Your mind is a battlefield where you have to take control of the opposition. Take advertising, for example, they plant a seed of thirst in you, longing to be satisfied, and before you know it, you're out in the stores or shopping online buying their product. Manufacturers are vying for possession of your mind and money by appealing to your appetite. The grim reality is the saying, "sex sells." Men and Women yield their bodies to viewing enticing audiences, incite appetites promoted by sinful desires, all in the name of a product. Developers spend millions of dollars on advertising because they have studied the human brain and know how it responds to different enticements.

Why would Paul make such a statement, *"Let this mind be in you which was also in Christ Jesus?"* Without the mind of Christ becoming your mind, you'll never be able to *"unplug."* To have the mind of Christ, you have to draw from the resource that fed the mind of Christ, which is the Word of God. *Plugging* into the Word is the only way to have the mind of Christ. You have to cut the cord from social resources, not because they are altogether wrong, but they cannot be spiritual guides. Remember, this is a forty-day challenge to reinvigorate your spiritual walk.

Often in life, you hear people say they believe in God, yet they don't think you need a church or a Pastor for eternal life. That's great that you believe in God, but it's required to hear the Word of God, and typically that requires a church and a Pastor.

I'll never forget when my father-in-law was in the hospital recovering from major surgery, and the doctors had just amputated from the knee down on one of his legs. My Pastor had come to visit him. He prayed for my father-in-law and tried to encourage him, but he was distraught, rightfully so. My father-in-law told my Pastor that he had faith, to which my Pastor replied, *"I believe you do, but what is your faith based on?"* That was one of the most profound questions I've ever heard. At that moment, I asked myself the same question, and I'm going to ask you the same question. *"What are you basing your faith on?"* Are you basing your faith on what you watch on TV or read on the internet? Are you basing your faith on the news? What sources are you plugged into that is determining your faith?

There's a saying I've heard before that says, *"Knowledge cancels our faith."* However, knowledge only cancels out faith when placed at a higher value than God's Word. If the external voices of media, human reasoning, and fear are negating the inner voice that wants to trust God for everything, then it's time to cut the cord! This forty-day challenge is a test of faith. I want you to get stronger in God and your faith to increase in His Word. The Lord's goal for you is to *"Cut the Cord"* and *"Unplug"* from all other voices; his voice will be the only one you hear. Hearing His voice above your own is a challenge in itself. This is not something new. People are so used to relying on their own voice that to *"Unplug"* from it is challenging. If you genuinely want His Will and not yours, then your will must cease to be. The Apostles made a statement to the Lord and should resonate with all of us; *"Increase our faith."* It's going to take faith to *"cut the cord."*

God loves faith because it is complete trust in Him. In the eleventh chapter, Paul wrote in Hebrews 11, verse six, otherwise known as the faith chapter. *"That without faith, it is impossible to please God."* It's going to be faith that gives you the strength to pick up the scissors and *"cut the cord,"* Church is the place where you get that strength. Faith and the Church are inseparable. How can a person say that they have faith, yet they don't believe you have to go to church? I might be ruffling some feathers, but it must be told. Hebrews 10:25 enlightens us on the faithfulness to church service, *"Not forsaking the assembling of ourselves together, as the manner of some is; but exhorting one another: and so much the more, as ye see the day approaching."* I believe we are living in that day — the technological age. Listening to a message on the radio or the internet is fine, but it should never replace the church. It's one thing if you are physically incapable of driving yourself self to a congregation. It's another thing when you are just too lazy and would rather sit on the couch or sleep in instead of going to church.

The church is a place where your faith is increased by hearing God's Word. Paul, writing to the church in Rome, addresses unfaithfulness to church, yet still professing faith. *Romans 10:17, "faith cometh by hearing, and hearing by the word of God."* If you want your faith to grow and you are well able, you're going to have to take the necessary steps to conquer the demons that you're *"Plugged"* into. I urge and admonish you for the next forty days to commit to being faithful to your church. *"Plug"* into His Word and *"Unplug"* from your own thoughts.

Often one thinks their thoughts are right because he's intellectual, and they make sense to him. However, there is no spiritual faith when it's backed by the ideologies of humanism. Man elevates his ideas above the Word of God with such statements as *"I think"* and *"I feel."*

> *"For my thoughts are not your thoughts, neither are your ways my ways, saith the Lord. For as the heavens are higher than the earth, so are my ways higher than your ways, and my thoughts than your thoughts."*
> *– Isaiah 55:8-9*

Man's thoughts can only become like God's thoughts when they are *"plugged"* into the Word of God and *"unplugged"* from his reasoning. Isaiah gives the analogy, clearly showcasing the great divide between the two dogmas. Philosophies and the tenets of man give way to carnally minded thinking, negating faith in the Word of God.

THE DEFINITION OF "CARNAL" ACCORDING TO THAYER'S DEFINITION

Carnal: The flesh denotes mere human nature, the earthly nature of man apart from divine influence, and therefore prone to sin and opposed to God.

When you're *"plugged"* into influences and resources that dictate and control your thought process apart from God, you are carnal. The Bible does not leave one stone unturned, and it is evident in letting its readers know what it is to be carnally minded. The following verses clearly depict the nature of a carnally minded individual. *(reread the definition of carnal)*

> *The works of the flesh are manifest, which are these; Adultery, fornication, uncleanness, lasciviousness. Idolatry, witchcraft, hatred, variance, emulations, wrath, strife, seditions, heresies, Envyings, murders, drunkenness, revellings, and such like: of the which I tell you before, as I have also told you in time past, that they which do such things shall not inherit the kingdom of God."*
>
> *– Galatians 5:19-21*

Galatians gives you an excellent description of what it means to be carnal. This doesn't mean you have to live in this state, nor does it mean that God does not love you and that you can't be forgiven. It's a struggle to be spiritually minded when you are bombarded with all that comes across the Internet and the world news. No, I am not condemning social media or the internet. Like anything else, it's a tool that can be used for good or used for bad. I teach a men's bible study at an N.A. and A.A. treatment center on Tuesday evenings, and I gave an analogy that struck a chord with them. I told them to take a hundred dollars. They now had two options --either take that hundred dollars and do something profitable like making sure they had a roof over their head or take that same hundred dollars and do something wasteful like buying more drugs or alcohol. The money itself wasn't the problem; it was the choices they made. God is for prosperity. I shared with them that I was homeless, penniless, and didn't even have a car or anything at one point in my life. Faith in God's Word and faithfulness to His house turned all those things around in my life, and it will, for them too.

I am by no means trying to say that you need to eradicate the internet or social media platforms from your life. What I am saying is that for some, those very sources could be the reason they're struggling in their spiritual walk with God; if so, *it's time to cut the cord.* I'm posing a challenge to step back, *"unplug,"* get grounded, and jumpstart your spiritual awareness. Like, money, the internet, cars, guns, your mind is a tool. How you use it determines what the outcome will be. Allow me to take this one step further. *"For to be carnally minded is death, but to be spiritually minded is life and peace" (Romans 8:6).* As you can see, there are two choices *'death' and 'life.'* For example, Adam and Eve were warned of the severe consequences they would suffer if they ate from the "tree of knowledge of good and evil." Metaphorically speaking, life is a tree, and every day it is producing fruit. You decide whether you eat from the branches of death or life. They never died naturally, but they died spiritually when they ate from the fruit of their own ideas. If you feed this mind all the things that entice the flesh and its sensual desires, you will be spiritually dead and separated from God; like Adam and Eve, when they were driven out from the presence of God in the Garden of Eden. On the other hand, when you eat from the branches of the "tree of life" (God's Word), you become spiritually minded, yet this is a great fear for some. Why? Because *"unplugging"* from the "normal" way of life is dreadful. One of the greatest fears of man is the unknown. Fear is a cruel taskmaster; it holds so many captives and prohibits them from desiring peace of mind. Jesus made it His mission statement at His inauguration **"to set the captives free"** *(Luke 4:18).* The Lord wants to set you free, but for Him to do so, there is something you must do on your part --*"cut the cord."*

The journey of a thousand miles begins with a single step. Rebuke your fear and turn the page to start a mission that will transform your life, mind, and spirit and give you the peace you so badly desire--more importantly, a magnificent walk with the Lord!

CHAPTER 2

PEACE OF MIND AND "UNPLUGGED" FROM FEAR AND LEARNING TO TRUST AGAIN

"And unto man he said, Behold, the fear of the Lord, that is wisdom; and to depart from evil is understanding" (Job 28:28). This verse tells us we should have *"fear for the lord."* "Fear" meaning respect and awe for the Mighty God in creation. *"And "fear" not them which kill the body, but are not able to kill the soul: but rather "fear" him which is able to destroy both soul and body in hell" (Matthew 10:28).* This life is temporal, and Jesus holds the keys to the eternal; this puts things into a clearer perspective. The Psalmist writes, *"Blessed is the man that "feareth" the LORD, that delighteth greatly in his commandments. Wealth and riches shall be in his house: and his righteousness endureth forever." (Psalm 112:1,3).* This is a healthy *fear* and one that produces the blessings of the Lord in your life. It's the negative fear you must *"unplug"* from that paralyzes you in the prison of your mind.

Fear is one of the most significant obstacles that stand in the way of inner peace for so many people. People often mask fear with arrogance and haughtiness, while internally, they are tormented. There are so many crippling fears out there; fear of "what will they think of me," fear of failure, fear of disappointing your peers, just to name a few. In my later teenage years, writer confession, maybe my early twenties, my greatest fear was getting old. That may sound somewhat crazy, but it's the truth. I would observe the elderly and ponder their ways and become overwhelmed by their inability to be the person they once were. I was young, vibrant, and full of life, and to not be that person mortified me. The only consolation I had to this fear was that I lived a life fueled by drugs and alcohol. I had created a premonition that I would die young. I envisioned my death in a horrific car accident due to my reckless and self-abandoned ways; hence I would never get old.

My second greatest fear was going to hell. Talk about having messed up priorities! My parents lived in a home that used a wood-burning stove for heat in the winter. My bedroom was in the basement, along with the stove. I can remember coming home in the early morning hours after an evening of playing at a club or partying, and I would fill the empty cavity in the stove to keep the house warm. I can remember bending over to open the stove door and feeling the heat radiating off its metal exterior. As I open the stove's portal, an invisible surge of heat would engulf my face. As I peered into the stove, looking at the glowing embers, I vividly remember the conversation I would have within myself. *"Tom, you will someday spend your eternity in this unbearable heat. You're going to burn in this flame forever."* I would shudder at this thought, and it haunted me in those quiet moments of silence. Looking back, I understand this was the Lord speaking to me and trying to draw me towards Him, with the reality of my *fears,* a most certain fate. At that time, I wasn't ready to listen to His voice. I wasn't willing to surrender my will at that point in my life. I wanted to be a rock-star at all costs, even if it meant my soul and eternity; I wanted my will above His.

How to obtain *peace of mind* is a great riddle. There are different degrees of *peace of mind* because no two people are the same. Take children, for example. They learn from their peers and those around them. As children, they are shaped and formed by their environment and influence, whether good or bad. As those seeds of influence take root and begin to grow and mature, they develop into their character. I first-handedly witnessed this in my children.

Your fears become a byproduct of multiple experiences you've encountered throughout your life, and they have left you traumatized. For example, my grandma never wanted to learn how to drive because she was in a horrible car accident when she was younger, and it left her fearful of driving. Fear can be one of the hardest things to conquer in this life. Fear is one of the most captivating mental prisons that humanity is enslaved to. In general, I believe man wants *peace of mind* and seeks every avenue within his own means to obtain it. If you could put the remedy to fear in a bottle, manufacture it, and sell it, you'd be on the Forbes Fortune 500 list for sure. For many, finding *peace of mind* is a relentless pursuit in life. Sadly, most people spend their entire life trying to find *peace of mind* in monetary possessions. Hiding behind social status and living in a facade to cover up their fears, with pseudo arrogance, because they think and feel that *things* bring them peace and acceptance from their peers. Money can buy a car, a new house, and any natural thing you may desire, but money can't mend a broken heart; only God can.

Peace of mind is not having the nicest car, the biggest home, the best job, or going on extravagant vacations around the world. Those things are all beautiful in their proper perspective, but the things of this life will never bring you *the peace of mind* that can only come from God. You can search from one end of the world to the other, but you will not find it. "*Peace of Mind*" cannot be found in the natural. The answer is short but sweet, and the *peace of mind* you want can be found in one simple verse:

> "*Thou wilt keep him in perfect peace, whose mind is stayed on thee: because he trusteth in thee.*"
>
> — *Isaiah 26:3*

Trust conquers *fear* and brings peace. I once read a bumper sticker that said, *"No Jesus, No Peace, Know Jesus, Know Peace!"* It's hard to have *"Peace of Mind"* when you're *plugged* into and inundated with: bill collectors, vehicle problems, money problems, relationship problems, health problems, job problems, etc. The war begins the second you open your eyes and roll out of bed and step onto the battlefield of life. Perplexing times, political unrest, and daily toils can steal the *"Peace of Mind"* you desire to have with God. With the simple opening of an app, you can unleash a barrage of news flashes, bulletins, and global terrorism attacks that can invade your thoughts in the blink of an eye. Instantly you can be thrown into the insanity of what's going on around you. You become overwhelmed by what's happening globally, and from coast to coast, *fear* begins to rob your faith in God and trust in His Will for your life. When your mind begins to go off-course, and you *unplug* from The Word of God *(the very compass that leads and guides you)*, you begin to navigate by your feelings and emotions and every other thing; instead of the Word, you lose *"Pease of Mind."* Your trust in God begins to wane, and your situations in life and your failures negate His abilities. The failures of your children cause you to question yourself. The failures of your spouse and your marriage have you reeling and living in despair. The failures in your career can cause you to question your self-worth. This is a reality, and It becomes hard to find *"Peace of Mind"* in the restless storms of life.

In the sixth chapter, in the book of Mark, you'll find Jesus, and his disciples, trying to escape for some alone time. Yes, even the Lord needed to *"unplug"* from people. Exhausted from their ministry's daily grind and the masses' thronging, it had taken a toll on them, and it was time for a rest. Shortly after reaching their destination, what they thought would be a peaceful day came to an abrupt halt. Word got out where Jesus was, and the masses began pouring in. Jesus saw the masses and had compassion on them; He denied Himself and gave them what they had come seeking, His Word. The Lord taught all day long. When the disciples realized the nearest town was a good distance away, they recommended that the Lord send the multitudes away before it got too dark, so they could get something to eat. The Lord's reply was, *"Give them something to eat."*

Well, that's easier said than done. The number of men, not counting the women and children, was about five thousand, and with only five loaves and two fishes, this would hardly suffice such a demand to feed the multitude. Remember, His ways are higher than your ways, and His thoughts are higher than your thoughts. I can imagine the Apostles saying to themselves, *"How is He going to feed all these people with only five loaves and two fishes?"* Being *"plugged"* into your five senses at times will hijack and rob you of your miracle. *Peace of mind* was nowhere to be found; in fact, it was the complete opposite. But the Lord's next statement signified He had it all under control. ***"Make them all sit down,"*** in other words, *"I got this."* You need to tell yourself, *"God's Got This!"*

By the time it was all said and done, everybody had eaten their fill. There were twelve baskets of leftovers. The Lord always shines out in the most difficult moments in life, especially when you find yourself in a situation like the disciples, and the Lord commands you to *"Give them something to eat."*

It seems so convoluted in these moments for many, and at times myself included, to have faith. *"Feed all these people with only a couple of fish and a few loaves, yeah, right!"* Everyone is guilty. We've all had our *"yeah right,"* moments where we let *fear* cancel out our *faith*. One of the hardest *fears* to conquer is taking both hands off the wheel. So, now it's time to reach down into your basket of faith and grab a piece of bread and start handing it out. Remember, *"God's got this!"*

After the campsite church service was dismissed, the Lord walked the apostles down to the harbor, instructing them *"go to the other side before unto Bethsaida."* Unlike, His previous request to feed over 5,000 people with only five loaves and two fishes, this seemed nothing out of the ordinary.

Night had fallen, and systematically like a fine-tuned machine, they begin to row in the direction of Bethsaida. The ores' harmonized sound making their entry and exit out of the water clicked like a metronome keeping perfect time. Mark doesn't give you a time frame as to how long they may have been at sea; he simply tells us, *"when even was come, the ship was in the midst of the sea, and he (the Lord) was alone on the land."* But, something undeniable had occurred unto them all, the sudden temperature change. Being seasoned veterans of the sea, this could mean only one thing; a storm was heading their way.

Instinctively there are times in life when you know a storm is coming, and the only thing you can do is try to brace yourself for what is about to hit you, as was the case with the disciples. Sometimes, however, it comes out of nowhere, and you're caught entirely off guard. As the winds increased and rowing became more laborious, it was obvious a storm was settling in. This is my rendition of what I feel like the dialogue was among the disciples. In his narrative, Mark does not disclose that to us.

Peter: *"Do you feel that, James?"*

James: *"Yeah, I feel it."*

Peter: *"You know what that means?"*

John: *"A storm is brewing."*

James: *"Peter, what do you think we should do, we're not that far from shore; should we turn back?"*

Peter: *"I know we're not that far from shore, but the Lord said that he would meet us on the other side."*

John: *"We still have a ways to go, and I don't think we'll beat the storm."*

Peter: *"No, not at the rate the wind has increased, and given the distance, we still have to go, it's going to catch us."*

The words had barely got out of their mouth as the conversation ended, and the storm overtook them. Mother Nature unleashed her rage and was handing out a full measure of her fury. As the minutes seemed like hours, and the storm showed no signs of relenting, *fear* was squeezing her grip tighter and tighter as the Apostles labored to do the Lord's Will. The boat being tossed about as the waves crashed over the sides, and the winds were contrary to them. Yet, they still rowed in direct opposition to their flesh. They were rowing in obedience to the Word. This is a metaphor for life and how unexpectedly a storm can hit, and along with it comes *fear*.

Fear is a cruel captor that shows no mercy. Fear goes to the extreme, and fear thinks the worst. How many times have you started out your day tending to your business when suddenly, a storm hit out of nowhere? Instantly your mind goes racing. You've just been broadsided and never saw it coming to prepare yourself, and now you're reeling in confusion. You start questioning God. You start questioning yourself. You try to figure out why and what just happened. Your mind becomes a whirly maze of chaos; instantly, you're stressed out!

Caught in a raging storm, the disciples had to be wondering why the Lord would tell them to meet him on the other side if He knew this would happen. Sometimes, God has to send you into the storms of life to manifest your "*fears*" so you can learn to put your "*faith*" and "*trust*" in Him.

Faith and *trust* in Him and His Word *(they are inseparable)* will help you *unplug* from your *fears* and conquer them even when it seems impossible. Mark 6:48 tells you that "*The Lord saw them toiling in rowing.*" The word "*toiling*" jumped off the page at me. I never truly understood its definition. I thought it meant *to struggle or labor,* and it does to a degree, but its actual meaning is far greater. The word "*toiling*" means "*to torture, pain, vexed with a grievous pain.*" The Lord saw the Apostles in pain, grievously tortured, trying to fulfill His Word.

There are times in your life when you are toiling to live His Word that you question His Will in your life. It's when you find yourself in the cradle of a wave on a raging sea that you lose *peace of mind.* You become *plugged* into the storm you are in, and the helpless feeling of despair drowns you. Like the faithful God He is, Jesus comes walking on water amid the storm and says, *"Be of good cheer it is I; be not afraid."* Sometimes that's easier said than done. It's hard to be at peace when you feel like, at any moment, you could capsize.

You may be amazed that God would send you into a storm, but without fail, Jesus will come walking on water and cause a still to come that only He can bring. The Apostle Peter reminds us that it's part of the *unplugging* process to have *peace of mind, "to think it not strange concerning the fiery trial, which is to try your faith" (1 Peter 4:12).* The definition of *faith* in its rawest form is complete trust! The Lord met the disciples when it seemed like all hope was lost, it was 11:59, the clock was about to strike midnight, and the boat was about to sink. I have had God take me several times to that very hour in my life. Not because He wasn't able to deliver me sooner, but my faith had to grow in Him as the storms of life become more significant. How would you ever know God was a healer if you never had an illness or disease and had to be healed?

Faith is rugged and born out of the crucibles of obedience to the Word. Faith is put to the test when it's His will above yours. It's in those 11:59 moments of life, you lose *"Peace of Mind."* I didn't always trust God like I do now. My faith has grown in Him. For the last twenty-plus years of my life, I've submitted my will to His. I've had plenty of failures, but here's a secret you'll never lose if you never quit; despite how many times you fail, just get back up and keep going. Life is full of problems and trials on this journey to your home in the sky. Different trials call for different answers to solve various issues, and those answers are found in His Word. The Lord instructed His disciples on the facts of life; he tells them, *"these things I have spoken unto you, that in me ye might have peace. In the world ye shall have tribulation: but be of good cheer; I have overcome the world" (John 16:33).* In modern-day terminology, there is this thing called "Life," Jesus called it *"The World!"* Let me break it down for you in simple, easy-to-understand terms. *"Life isn't going to be easy or fair, and I never said it would be, but because I forewarned you, you can unplug" from the fear of situations. Have peace of mind. I told you tribulations will come, so don't act surprised when life gets crazy and throws you a curve-ball, but trust in Me!"*

FEAR IS REAL, AND THIS WORLD CAN BE A FEARFUL PLACE

In 2 Timothy, Paul writes to Timothy, instructing him on how to address *fear*. Apparently, the young minister may have been struggling with his own personal issues. Paul writes, *"For God hath not given us the spirit of fear, but of power, and of love, and of a sound mind"* *(2Timonty 1:7)*. We all have our personal problems, and for some, *fear* is a big one, and it encompasses many facets. Fear will rob your faith, joy, peace and will destroy your *trust* if you let it. Again, it's easier said than done, and to *unplug* from it takes time. The previous verse tells you how to overcome --*" but of power, and of love, and of a sound mind."* God hasn't given you the spirit of *fear* but power. The power of God is the Spirit of God. The Love of God is, He's with you every step of the way as you walk in His Will. The infusion of the two igniting produces a sound mind or simply *Peace of Mind*.

Your body and the way God has created it is a wonder. Your ability is utterly amazing. Your body and its emotions release hormones for every situation you experience. Scientists say the reason you can remember things from your childhood that reach back fifty to sixty years is the emotions attached to them, good or bad. Chemicals are released in your body that trigger emotions that leave indelible marks. *Fear* is one of them. Fear releases a hormone in your body called adrenaline. In *"fight or flight"* situations, this hormone surges through your body, causing high blood pressure and an increased heart rate. Sadly, some people live their life in a constant *"fight or flight'* mode reaping havoc on their bodies. The woes of this life can cause a spirit of *fear* to grip you, and you find yourself trapped in the *"fight or flight"* mode on a perpetual basis.

Murder is real. Hard times are real. People standing on the street corners with signs, saying *"will work for food are real."* Pain caused by hatred and the color of the skin is real. Your personal pain is real. *Fears* will try to cause you to doubt God and question your faith in His Word. Not being able to pay bills is fearful. Wondering how you're going to put food on the table for your family is a dreadful thing. In this life, you will have tribulation, but be of good cheer; God uses all things as part of the refining process to give you the *peace of mind* you desire. Remember, you would never know He was able unless you were unable.

The Lord didn't call you to be fearful, but He called you to be a soldier who stands firm in the face of adversity. Why? Because you are *plugged* into His Word, knowing God's got your back because you trust Him. The Apostle Paul admonishes you with eight simple words, and so do I; *"We walk by faith, not by sight" (2 Corinthians 5:7).* *"Fear"* is the absence of faith, and faith is the absence of fear. The world is watching to see what you're *plugged into* --fear or faith?

A mighty nation's birth started out with the call and a promise to one man, and that man was Abraham. Your walk with the Lord started out with a call and a promise, like Abraham. You don't know precisely where God will lead your life or how long it's going to take to get there.

Abraham, who just had God appear to him out of nowhere, most likely had some fears. Fear of the unknown. Fear of the what-ifs? Fear of separation from friends and family. Fear was at every turn as Abraham faced the unknown. However, Abraham's faith to trust God was greater than the fear of doubting God's plan. You have to have faith and believe in God and His calling in your life. Your greatness begins with stepping out and *unplugging from fear*. Abraham's greatness wouldn't entirely be seen until generations down the road, in the miraculous deliverance of his great, great-grandchildren, from their Egyptian bondage. Sometimes your greatness isn't revealed until later in life. Why? Because God is setting things up in your life for great deliverance, like the children of Israel. In Abraham's life, you can see his fears take control because he stopped walking by faith and allowed his sight to dictate.

> *And there was a famine in the land: and Abram went down into Egypt to sojourn there; for the famine was grievous in the land.*
>
> *And it came to pass, when he was come near to enter into Egypt, that he said unto Sarai his wife, "Behold now, I know that thou art a fair woman to look upon:*
>
> *Therefore it shall come to pass, when the Egyptians shall see thee, that they shall say, This is his wife: and they will kill me, but they will save thee alive.*
>
> *Say, I pray thee, thou art my sister: that it may be well with me for thy sake; and my soul shall live because of thee."*
>
> *And it came to pass, that, when Abram was come into Egypt, the Egyptians beheld the woman that she was very fair.*
>
> *The princes also of Pharaoh saw her, and commended her before Pharaoh: and the woman was taken into Pharaoh's house.*
>
> *— Genesis 12:10-18*

The famine was a setup, just like when the Lord told the disciples, *"go to the other side before unto Bethsaida."* It's a setup. God set Abraham up. Don't get offended by this because maybe now you realize God has set you up, but He had to. It's part of the process of *unplugging*. Situations in life can bring things inside of you to the surface, things that you may have never realized were there until a storm hits. The Lord saw the disciples suffering while trying to fulfill His Word. God saw the *fear* that riddled

Abraham when he realized that his life was possibly threatened. Abraham had just started walking with God in the 12ᵗʰ Chapter of Genesis, and he's already being tested. Sometimes it hits hard and fast, and I don't know why except for the fact that God knows exactly what's best for you. Why did Abraham lie? The same reason every one of us lies, fear. You're afraid to get caught because of the consequences of your actions. In Abraham's case, he was scared they would kill him for his wife. Yet, God's divine mercy overshadowed Abraham's *fear*.

We'll give Abraham a pass here --he was a young Christian who just started walking with God, but what about twenty-four years later, when he faced the same trial? Surely, by now, as a mature saint and the father of faith, he would pass the same test with flying colors, right? Wrong.

> *And Abraham journeyed from thence toward the south country, and dwelled between Kadesh and Shur, and sojourned in Gerar.*
> *And Abraham said of Sarah his wife, "She is my sister:" and Abimelech king of Gerar sent, and took Sarah.*
> *– Genesis 20:1-2*

Sometimes it takes years to overcome certain personal struggles and *Unplugging* from *Fear* takes time. Here you see Abraham facing the same dilemma that he did twenty-four years earlier, and again he fails along with his faith. However, this time, God visits Abimelech in a dream, telling him, *"if you even think about touching this woman, thou are but a dead man."* Abimelech, taken completely aback, not only by the visitation from God but the sharp rebuke, informing him that his very life could have been taken out because he has another man's wife.

> *Therefore Abimelech rose early in the morning, and called all his servants, and told all these things in their ears: and the men were sore afraid.*

Then Abimelech called Abraham, and said unto him, "What hast thou done unto us? and what have I offended thee, that thou hast brought on me and on my kingdom a great sin? thou hast done deeds unto me that ought not to be done."

And Abimelech said unto Abraham, "What sawest thou, that thou hast done this thing?"

And Abraham said, "Because I thought, Surely the fear of God is not in this place; and they will slay me for my wife's sake."

— Genesis 20:8-11

What prompted Abraham to say, *"I thought the Fear of God is not in this place,"* was his own fear. *Fear* can cause you to respond and say certain things because you have no *Peace of Mind*. Without peace of mind, we can make knee-jerk decisions that lead to more heartache and pain.

Fast forward several years, and you see a different Abraham. This time Abraham has *Unplugged* from his *Fears;* he's walking in *Peace of Mind* and the confidence of God on his side, leading and guiding his life. The blessings of God were abounding in every area of Abraham's life. Isaac, their promised son, had grown and become a young man learning the art of agriculture and raising livestock. Abraham had a sincere walk with God, a prayer life, and was devoted to giving God his absolute best. Even though he may have failed at times, Abraham never staggered at the promises of God but was strong in faith.

One day, Abraham's faith would be put to the ultimate test, and not only his faith but Isaac's faith too. The setting is not revealed, nor do we know the time of day or the circumstances surrounding the event. My best guess would be after Abraham had offered God a sacrifice. Watching as the fire and smoke ascended, his thoughts were interrupted by the familiar voice that had called him over twenty-five years ago.

And it came to pass after these things, that God did tempt Abraham, and said unto him, "Abraham," and he said, "Behold, here I am."

And he said, "Take now thy son, thine only son Isaac, whom thou lovest, and get thee into the land of Moriah; and offer him there for a burnt offering upon one of the mountains which I will tell thee of."

— *Genesis 22:1-2*

Speechless. The scripture never indicates nor insinuates that Abraham responded verbally to God's sinful request. Human sacrifice was only a practice heathens performed as they offered their young to Molech and Baal's gods. Disheveled by such a request, Abraham doesn't repeat the matter to Sarah. Surely, she would have none of it. You can't tell people some things because they will try to discourage you from doing what God has called you to. It's between you and God. The definition of "faith" is complete trust. Abraham trusted God, and so must you. *"Trust in the LORD with all thine heart; and lean not unto thine own understanding"* (Proverbs 3:5).

Abraham wanted to tell Sarah what God had told him, but he couldn't. His heart was broken, and his *peace of mind* was fleeing, and Abraham's *Fears* came to life. If he told Sarah, a war would ensure, and God never mentioned bringing Sarah, just Isaac. Besides, it would be too much for her to bear, watching him offer up their son as a burnt sacrifice to God.

I'm going to insert what I believe the conversation might have been between Abraham and Sarah. As she walked into the tent, and found Abraham packing his bags.

Abraham: *"Good evening, Sarah."*
Sarah: *"Good evening Abraham, what's going on? Why are you packing your bags?"*

Abraham: *"God has called Isaac, and myself to go offer a sacrifice unto Him in an unknown mountain."*

Sarah: *"Abraham, you seem troubled. Is something wrong?"*

Abraham *"No, nothing is wrong."*

Sarah: *"Are you sure, Abraham, nothing is wrong? I've never seen you look so downhearted going to meet God for a sacrifice, do you want me to go with you?"*

Abraham: *"I'm okay, trust me, nothing is wrong. No, the Lord only told me to bring Issac. I'm not sure when I'll be home, but we'll see you soon."*

Sarah: *"Okay, Abraham, I trust you. If God has called you to sacrifice, you must go."*

Abraham: *"I love you, Sarah. I'm going to retire early tonight. We have to be up at first light. Good night Sarah."*

Sarah: *"Good night Abraham, I love you too."*

> *Abraham rose up early in the morning, and saddled his ass, and took two of his young men with him, and Isaac his son, and clave the wood for the burnt offering, and rose up, and went unto the place of which God had told him.*
>
> *Then on the third day Abraham lifted up his eyes, and saw the place afar off.*
>
> *And Abraham said unto his young men, "Abide ye here with the ass; and I and the lad will go yonder and worship, and come again to you."*
>
> *– Genesis 22:3-5*

It's time to trust in the Lord and lean not unto your own understanding. You must venture to your yonder and face your fears if you want to have the *Peace of Mind* you so desperately want. But, for some, it comes with a high price, and that price is stepping out and trusting God. *Trust* may be one of the biggest things you struggle with. The *Fear* of letting down your walls and letting God in is overwhelming. Your trust in people has been destroyed, and you're having a hard time trusting the Lord; you are not alone. The Psalmist David, in his writing, assures you that it is possible to trust the Lord. *"Trust in him at all times; ye people, pour out your heart before him: God is a refuge for us" (Psalms 62:8).* Pour your heart out to Him. Let God know all your hurts…your pains…and the struggle you have with trust so that he can help you to trust again. The word *refuge means hope, shelter, and trust.* Those words are what God is when you start to *Trust* Him. Jubilation will break forth in your soul, and God's Spirit will sweep through you as the walls come down and His presence comes in. But, it will never happen unless you take that first step towards the place God has called you; you must go yonder.

Job, a man acquainted with sorrows, penned a beautiful scripture depicting faith above fear and trust beyond circumstance, *"Though he slay me, yet will I trust in him" (Job 13:15).* Job lost everything dear to him --his children, his friends, his livelihood, his health, he even had to endure the scorn of his wife. Albeit, he still trusted the Lord. To relinquish the reservations, you hold in your heart that is enshrouded in pain is inconceivable. We often cling to the familiar because the fear of the unfamiliar is paralyzing. Sadly, this becomes what I call security in bondage. God has offered you a way of escape by trusting Him, but you remain a prisoner to your pain when you don't take advantage of it.

Take the children of Israel, for example. They had been slaves for hundreds of years. All they ever knew was bondage in Egypt. Many years had passed since Joseph was a ruler, and the freedom they once knew was long gone. Without going into a lengthy soliloquy about the life of Moses, I will share with you what God spoke to him at the burning bush, *"I have surely seen the affliction of my people which are in Egypt, and have heard their cry by reason of their taskmasters; for I know their sorrows. And I am come down to deliver them out of the hand of the Egyptians, and to bring them up out of that land unto a good land and a large, unto a land flowing with milk and honey" (Exodus 3:7-8).* God has seen your affliction, heard your cry, and He knows your sorrow. He wants to bring you out of the bondage you think is security. Israel gives you insight into how, after years of slavery, pleasure and pain had become the same. As bad as they wanted to get out, and as much as they hated the sting of the whip, it had become a way of life. Because along with the beatings came the provisions that sustained their lives, and a sickening co-dependent had formed.

Their food, income, and everything they had come to know were provided by Egypt. You may be in an abusive relationship, and as much as you want to leave, it's what you've come to know as life, but that's not a life that anybody should have. It's time to break the chains of mental slavery that has you bound and get out of that abusive co-dependent re-lationship --God's got better things in store for your life. With God, all things are possible.

Just after God brings the children of Israel out of four-hundred years of slavery, with one of the most remarkable deliverances ever witnessed *(the ten plagues),* one would think that their faith was on such a high that no one, or nothing, could stand in their way, right? Wrong! The long-term effects of abuse on individuals' minds, who have lived at the hands of their abusers, are staggering. They become anesthetized to the pain, and when forced to step into the unknown and unfamiliar, they revert back to the self-surrendered sickening, abusive lifestyle for relief. At the first impasse *(the Red Sea),* what is the first thing Israel says? *"And they said unto Moses, Because there were no graves in Egypt, hast thou taken us away to die in the wilderness? wherefore hast thou dealt thus with us, to carry us forth out of Egypt? Is not this the word that we did tell thee in Egypt, saying, Let us alone, that we may serve the Egyptians? For it had been better for us to serve the Egyptians, than that we should die in the wilderness" (Exodus 14:11-12).*

"Let us alone, that we may serve the Egyptians? For it had been better for us to serve the Egyptians than that we should die in the wilderness." Are

you kidding me? Let us go back to Egypt! Israel believed they were better off living at the hands of their abusers and the comfort of knowing their lives were being provided for than to face the uncertainty of trusting God. Please, don't let this become your thinking during this journey. I'm imploring you. You know God delivered Israel from the hands of their oppressors, and God will deliver you from yours. Remember to have *Peace of Mind* and *Unplugged* from *Fear;* you have to *Trust* the Lord.

> *And Abraham said unto his young men, "Abide ye here with the ass; and I and the lad will go yonder and worship, and come again to you." And Abraham took the wood of the burnt offering, and laid it upon Isaac his son; and he took the fire in his hand, and a knife; and they went both of them together.*
>
> *And Isaac spake unto Abraham his father, and said, "My father": and he said, "Here am I, my son." And he said, "Behold the fire and the wood: but where is the lamb for a burnt offering?"*
>
> *And Abraham said, "My son, God will provide himself a lamb for a burnt offering:" so they went both of them together.*
>
> *And they came to the place which God had told him of; and Abraham built an altar there, and laid the wood in order, and bound Isaac his son, and laid him on the altar upon the wood.*
>
> *And Abraham stretched forth his hand, and took the knife to slay his son.*
>
> *— Genesis 22:5-10*

I have read and heard this story hundreds of times, and every time I am moved to tears. You cannot tell me that Abraham wasn't sobbing as he looked into the eyes of his terrified son, Isaac, as he bound him on the altar, and as he grasped the knife in obedience to God, to slay the very promise he had waited twenty-five years for. Talk about the ultimate test of *faith* and *trust,* the apex of yonder was at center stage --Abraham's next move was the ending of Isaac's life.

> *And the angel of the LORD called unto him out of heaven, and said, "Abraham, Abraham:" and he said, "Here am I."*
> *And he said, "Lay not thine hand upon the lad, neither do thou any thing unto him: for now I know that thou fearest God, seeing thou hast not withheld thy son, thine only son from me."*
> *And Abraham lifted up his eyes, and looked, and behold behind him a ram caught in a thicket by his horns: and Abraham went and took the ram, and offered him up for a burnt offering in the stead of his son.*
> *— Genesis 22:6-13*

It may have been a three-day journey to reach the mountain God called Abraham to, but it took twenty-five years of walking with God to prepare Abraham for his yonder experience. God has been preparing you and calling you on this journey for quite a while so that you can not only have the *peace of mind* you want but the ability to *trust* again. Abraham displayed the ultimate faith in God by *trusting* and committing to the unthinkable. As you read this, there may be some things that you feel God is telling you to offer up, and it's inconceivable in your mind. Remember that your mind has been your enemy this whole time. Push those thoughts out and take the first step *to peace of mind* by *unplugging.* God met Abraham and He'll meet you too.

CHAPTER 3

SOMETIMES YOU HAVE TO HIT ROCK BOTTOM BEFORE YOU CAN "UNPLUG"

And he would fain have filled his belly with the husks that the swine did eat: and no man gave unto him. And when he came to himself, he said, How many hired servants of my father's have bread enough and to spare, and I perish with hunger!

– Luke 15:16-17

As the chapter title states, having to hit rock bottom is a harsh and brutal truth. Sadly, for some (myself included), this has to become the starting point. I have a very addictive personality, and I'm an extremist by default. Everything I get into, I go all out; it's a hundred or nothing. Those of you that can relate are probably laughing right now to yourself, saying, *"yep, that's me."* An addictive personality is not necessarily a bad trait. It only becomes a curse when you direct all that desire in the wrong direction. In 1 Corinthians 16:16, Paul stated: *"the house of Stephanas had addicted themselves to the ministry of the saints."* I wish my addiction started out like Stephanas's, but unfortunately, it wasn't even close.

I don't think nobody ever starts out in life wanting to become an addict. I have never heard a child say, *"When I grow up, I want to become a heroin addict or a crack addict, or an alcoholic, or a foodie."* For some, I believe it's not so much that they have an addictive personality, but it is an escape from a painful situation or wanting acceptance from peers that drives them. There is a certain kinship amongst addicts. Their storylines often run parallel. Divorced homes or abusive homes (*mentally or physically*), high school dropouts, or parents that struggled with substance abuse themselves. Unfortunately, their children often follow suit and travel down the same path. It's a traumatic environment for a child to grow up in and develop.

Ray, a very dear friend of mine, who I attend church with, has a similar story of those who follow the wrong path. His father passed at the age of thirty-five when Ray was only seven. His mother did her best to raise him and his siblings in a good home. However, by the time Ray reached his teenage years, he was using drugs and alcohol. This would lead Ray down a very dark road. He became addicted to crack-cocaine, and his addiction took him to places he never imagined he would go. Ray's addiction became so bad that he turned to crime to finance his over-the-top addiction. Ray would go on a crime spree that would see him commit over 300 breaking and enterings!

Ray shared a story with me about an incident that happened to him when he was driving through a very rough part of Detroit. The area is laden with abandoned cars on the streets, burned-out homes, vacant lots with the grass overgrown where homes once stood. Ray had been up for nine days straight, committed multiple robberies, and needed more dope. He approached a man on the street about purchasing drugs; things didn't go very well, they got into a verbal altercation; as Ray pulled away, he heard a gunshot. As he drove around the block, Ray began to feel something warm running down the side of his face; Ray had been shot. He pulled over, looked in the rearview mirror, and saw a bullet lodge in his forehead, at the base of his hairline. Enraged at what had just happened, Ray went back looking for the man who had just shot him, but he was nowhere to be found. Before the night was over, Ray would find himself behind bars and lucky to be alive.

Ray would see multiple times of incarceration for D.U.I. and lose his license for over twenty years. This type of addictive reckless lifestyle carried on for decades until one day, his brother, who had struggled with addiction himself, invited Ray to our church.

Ray started attending church, got his life back on track, and met his future wife, Nancy. Nancy also had struggles with addiction in her past. Even though Ray had gotten his life back on track, Ray had not hit *Rock Bottom* yet and was by no means ready to *Unplug*. The bottom wouldn't come for a while, but he wasn't alone when it did; Nancy came with it.

Unlike Ray, Nancy came from a very well-to-do family from Grosse Pointe, MI. Nancy's father had many successful businesses. The family had a cabin up north, and monetary wants were never issues. The only want Nancy had in her life was her father's love and acceptance.

Nancy was different from her other siblings --she had a weight problem. Her weight issues became her father's mission to get rid of. His mission would only fuel Nancy's food addiction. It drove a wedge in the relationship between her and her father. Her father's frustration with her inability to lose weight caused him to become cruel and hurtful to Nancy. In his relentless attempts to help control her weight loss, he would go to extremes. He would reduce her daily food allowance and put her on regular exercise programs that he would monitor. This type of abuse only propelled Nancy deeper into her food addiction. Food became the only comfort she had. She would sneak downstairs at night when everybody was sleeping and take food from the cupboards, hiding it in her room where she would binge.

Struggling to lose weight to make her father happy and trying to find acceptance within herself, Nancy lived in an internal nightmare that she couldn't wake up from. Why couldn't she be like her siblings? They didn't struggle with weight. They didn't have to have food reductions. They weren't made to feel less than because of how they looked. The only comfort Nancy had was the very thing she was battling (*food*). Wanting to be loved for who she was, and not who she was supposed to be, would be the fuel to a crack addiction that would drag her into a rabbit hole in her attempts to escape the pain.

By the time she was in high school, Nancy had started smoking cigarettes and was experimenting with drinking and smoking marijuana. Still, food was her drug of choice.

At home, the constant pressure from her father to lose weight was mounting. The war raging inside her head was taking new heights, and the summer after she graduated would change her life forever.

After babysitting one night for a friend, that friend returned home with another couple. They asked Nancy if she wanted to get high. It wasn't marijuana they would be smoking; it was crack-cocaine. Nancy had never smoked crack-cocaine before, and her decision to start that night would be the beginning of a six-year addiction that would end with her behind bars.

Nancy finally *hit rock bottom* and was ready to *"unplug"* from her addiction. After several rehab centers, Nancy finally got clean at twenty-three and maintained her sobriety for twelve years. N.A. would be a springboard for Nancy's spiritual awakening. A friend would invite her to a Bible study, and that Bible study would change her life forever.

Nancy started attending Bible study, and shortly after that, she started going to church. Things began to change in her appearance and her speech. Nancy was changed, and all those around her noticed. For the first time in a long time, Nancy had found joy beyond the freedom of being clean from drugs.

I can remember Nancy telling Laura and myself that God had shown her that Ray would be her husband (in my mind, I couldn't see it). Meanwhile, Ray had stopped going to church and had fallen back into his addiction. Nancy remained faithful to church, but still struggling with wanting the love she had never gotten from her father, she started pursuing Ray. It didn't take much time before Nancy had fallen back into addiction with Ray and left the church.

It would be three years, tens of thousands of dollars later, having escaped being chased by drug dealers and the countless time they could have overdosed from the copious amounts of crack they consumed before they really *Hit Rock Bottom* and were ready to *unplug*.

It's been well over a decade since they both have been back in church, married, and on fire for God. God has blessed their lives in so many ways. Nancy has taken on a burden for those still suffering from addiction, and she has gotten involved with a local program called "Hope not Handcuffs." Nancy had reached out to treatment centers, and through her, God has made way for me to go into a treatment center and teach weekly Bible studies to men. Let God turn your story into His glory. *"Rock Bottom"* is not the end but a new beginning.

Nancy had been an acquaintance with my wife Laura's family; Jodie, Laura's younger sister, and Nancy were in the same grade. Like Nancy, Laura was also raised in Grosse Pointe, MI. Her grandfather had a highly successful family tool and die business, and they lived in a beautiful home. Laura's parents got divorced when she was twelve years old. Their divorce would be the springboard for Laura's addiction and a whirlwind of misery and chaos that would envelop her life. Laura's dad, Bob, was a great father to his children and provided a comfortable lifestyle, with one exception --he was a raging gambler.

Bob's addiction to dice, cards, and the racetrack would be the ruin of their home. It would be a divorce that Laura and her sisters would endure for seven long years. The destruction of her parent's marriage ignited a rebellion inside of Laura with an *"I don't care attitude."*

By the time Laura was twenty, she had gone to jail, wrecked several cars, and encountered many woes for such a young age. During the divorce, her mother had become an alcoholic, and her home life was a tumultuous sea. One night while Laura was out on a binge herself, she had a blackout, and when she woke up, she was in jail. The horrifying reality of being in jail and not knowing if she had killed somebody in her drunken recklessness was mortifying. Fortunately for Laura, she didn't kill anyone. She had only passed out while driving, and her car was parked on the median. Laura had finally *Hit Rock Bottom* and was ready to *Unplug* from the bondage of drugs and alcohol that was destroying her life.

By this time, her mother had gotten sober also and had started attending A. A. meetings. A. A. would be the place where Laura would find sobriety and a new lease on life. However, sobriety doesn't always mean peace. Laura's life continued to have one woe after another. Her boyfriend would be murdered by a rival drug lord who had put a hit on him. He was sitting at a stoplight in her car when he was gunned down. Unbeknownst to Laura, her boyfriend was a drug-dealer, and the Chaldean mafia paid his friends $5,000.00 to have him killed. With what seemed like one plague after another in her life, she couldn't figure out why the insanity hadn't stopped?

Life seemed unfair, and if things could and would go wrong, they did. Laura had *"Hit Rock Bottom"* again. Sobriety couldn't do it, men couldn't do it, socializing couldn't do it. Because of N.A. and A.A., Laura and Nancy had come into contact again, and their friendship had grown. Laura watched Nancy's transformation; she saw the joy Nancy had and that she didn't. So, when Nancy invited her to a Bible study, she was ready to *unplug*.

It was 1991 when Laura went to the Bible study, and not long after she was in the Bible study, Laura woke up one Sunday morning and decided she was going to go to Nancy's church. Born and raised Catholic, Laura attended mass on and off throughout her life, but there was something different about Nancy's church and what she was learning in the Bible study. She said within herself, *"What do I have to lose?"* Her life felt unfulfilled and without purpose, and for the first time in her life, God seemed to have a purpose.

Laura attended the morning church service, and it was like nothing she had ever experienced in her life. The worship was amazing, and the preacher was unlike any preacher she had ever heard before. Not only was he preaching about the God Laura was learning about in the Bible study, but he was also preaching about her life without even knowing her.

She ended up attending the evening service, and that evening God would fill her with His Spirit. She would be baptized in His name, washing away all the sins of her past. Laura was born again and has never wavered in her dedication to the Lord.

There is a phrase in N. A. that is known as *"a trigger!"* A trigger is something that sparks the flames of addiction back up in someone and causes them to relapse. A trigger can also ignite a flame inside a person that they weren't even aware existed.

I will rewind the tape a bit here and delve back into my early childhood, where my addictive personality first manifests itself. As I am sitting here writing, the image is clearly etched into my mind. Although the store has been closed for several decades, the picture and sound of the creaking, 21/4" wooden floors are still very vivid. As you approached the entrance to the store, the redolent smell of popcorn hung in the air. I'll never forget the sound of the bells ringing that was draped from the handle on the door as you opened it, signifying a customer had just entered the store. It was down the center aisle of *Gamble's,* the local hardware/general store located in Imlay City, MI., where the life-altering incident would occur. As you entered the store halfway down the central aisle, was a record shelf on the left. As my mother and I strolled past it, I saw something so awe-striking it paralyzed me in my tracks. Its image was haunting and yet captivating. There, staring at me, and I back at them, was my trigger; it was the double album Kiss Alive II. With the four band members' faces on its cover, its image was unlike any other.

Their faces were painted with white make-up, and in black, were precise lines drawn, carefully detailing the portrait of a mystical creature that had possessed them. The image of Gene Simons, as the demon with blood all over his face, handcuffed me to the place I was standing. Next to Gene was Paul Stanley, the star child, and the other two members. I was imprisoned with wonderment. Who were they? Who was this band called "Kiss," and what was their music like? I stared at the album cover the entire time we were in the store. I was eaten up with curiosity about these four mystical creatures that had just enslaved my attention. My mother pulled me from my statuesque pose as she let the store.

The following days and weeks after my encounter with the album cover would be my thoughts' devotion. I had to have this album at all costs (this should have been a sign to my parents that their son was an addict, I was around 7-8). Easter was just around the corner, and I reminded my mom about the album I had seen at the store several weeks ago. I knew if I pestered my mom long enough, she would get it for me. Every Easter, she would get us gifts and put them in our baskets.

Easter Sunday came, and before anybody was up, I was headed for the table. The excitement of getting the album and the fear of not getting it was somewhat traumatizing. Inside, I knew my mom would grant me my burning desire, and it would be waiting for me. As I approached the table, I stopped dead in my tracks, and the same four mystical faces that were staring at me in the store were now looking back at me, only this time it was from the kitchen table. I snatched it from the basket and dashed off to my bedroom. I plopped down on my bed and just stared at it. The album was wrapped in cellophane, so I couldn't feel its texture; I had to remove this thin transparent barrier that separated me from it.

What lay between those two covers would change my life forever and trigger a passion so deep inside me that I would follow it at all costs! As I opened the double live album, its contents left me speechless. I had never seen anything like it before

There they were, this band called *Kiss* decked out in full regalia. The image was staggering. They were elevated several feet in the air, and the drummer was perched high above the stage on a riser. There was a set of staircases on each side of the drums leading down to the stage floor. All the pyrotechnics were going off simultaneously. Flames were shooting up from the stage; there was a thick haze of smoke above the floor. I was utterly captivated. At that very moment, in a trice second, I told myself, "I'm going to be a Rockstar!"

I come from a musical background, so I had something's working in my favor to help me achieve this newfound dream. My father played guitar casually, but my grandfather was a devoted musician. There was an old acoustic guitar lying around the house that I would mess with; I would put that "Kiss" record on and air guitar every song on that live album. I would imagine myself playing those guitar solos, and the sound of the crowd in between songs told me, "One day, those will be your accolades." It would be well over a decade before that dream ever became a reality.

I left home at seventeen and had to quit school because I had no legal guardianship. I was on my own, and the world was taking on a new form. This really was the beginning of my addiction to drugs and alcohol. If I wanted to do something, I just did it. I had a false sense of liberation. At this point in my life, I had not wholeheartedly devoted myself to music yet. Living on my own and partying was at center stage. One day Bill, a good friend of mine, asked me if I wanted to form a band with him and this drummer he knew, so the obvious answer was YES!

We learned a few songs, but I wasn't really dedicated to making it a band. The chemistry with those guys wasn't there, and our musical differences were apparent. I wanted to play fast metal stuff, and they wanted to play more of a blues-oriented style. I enjoyed the fun of it. It was a great learning experience, but it wasn't anything that I would seriously commit to.

God is an omi-present God; He's working, even when you think He isn't, He is. It was Bill's seventeenth birthday, and his parents said we could have a party and invite people over and jam. I guess this was technically my first public appearance as a guitar player, and I thought I was a Rockstar. It was a lot of fun, an acquaintance from school was there watching us jam. He wanted to learn how to play guitar and asked if I would show him a few things, and naturally, I said yes. His name was Bayn, and we would become best friends, bandmates, and brothers in the Lord down the road. After hanging out a few times and showing Bayn some stuff on the guitar, he suggested that we take lessons; brilliant, I thought. I had just moved back home to my Mom's house. I had quit Bill's band and now had a place where I could practice and get serious about my playing without being interrupted.

As the lessons progressed, so did my playing. My desire was more alive than ever. I began to live, eat, sleep, and drink music, and so did Bayn. We immersed ourselves in anything and everything that had to do with playing guitar.

My addictive personality went into overdrive, and everything else went out the window. I decided I wouldn't work anymore and devote all my time to perfecting my playing; however, my mother wasn't all for it. After months of telling me to get a job, which I completely ignored, I came home one day to an unpleasant surprise. In the middle of the driveway was a pile of all my clothes and my guitar. Attached to my possessions was a note that read,

"Because you refuse to get a job and no longer want to be responsible, you can no longer live here."
— Mom

I was homeless, without a job, and penniless. Most would consider this *"Hitting Rock Bottom."* One would think the sensible thing to do would be to tell your Mom, "*I'm sorry, please give me another chance, I'll get a job, don't kick me out.*" Wrong! I said, "Okay, I'll figure it out." That night I slept on Bayn's parent's couch. It just so happened I knew Bayn's aunt very well, and I ended up moving in with her.

I cut the grass and did other chores for my keep. She agreed to pay for my lessons and gave me a little extra to live on until I got a job. Bayn was laid off from work at the time, so we spent 4-6 hours everyday practicing. After several months of lessons, my playing had advanced rather quickly. We didn't have jobs to work, so practicing became our job. After practice was done, the evening would come, and so did the drugs and alcohol; it was time to party.

I soon realized if you want to be a Rockstar, you have to have the equipment, and making twenty-five dollars a week to live on wasn't going to cut it. I had moved back in with my Mom at the end of that summer due to some crazy drug-related circumstances that transpired while living at Bayn's aunts. By this time, I had gotten a job and a car.

My circle of friends had become all musicians; through a mutual friend, I was invited to play with a group of guys putting together a band. We jammed together all day and hit it off great. By the end of the night, they asked me if I wanted to form a band with them. These guys were not like Bill and Dave, they were dedicated to their craft, and we shared the same musical taste. Everything fit like a hand and glove, and what I had been dreaming about since the day I first opened up that Kiss Alive II album, was coming to pass. I finally was on my way to becoming a Rockstar. I said yes, and from that point on, we became a family: Pete, Tony, Stacy, Tim, and I were an official band. Our passions were united, and life was all about music and becoming Rockstars.

We always rehearsed constantly, learning all our favorite songs, and we had our sights on playing anywhere and everywhere. People just started showing up at practices, wanting to hang out with us. It was a surreal moment for me. Given my personality and addictive nature, it didn't take long for me to adopt the "Rockstar" attitude and the "Rockstar" lifestyle of constant playing, excessive drinking, and partying.

I never really was a big drinker up until this point in my life. The drug of choice at the time was marijuana. I experimented with various drugs for a short period of time, but I soon realized that it would be my dreams' demise, so I quit. Before we knew it, we were playing at parties and small clubs, and everywhere we could. Alcohol was in a perpetual flow, and the day came that I actually wanted a drink more than a drug; then and there, I realized I had procured an addiction to alcohol.

Over a year had passed since the first day that we formed the band. The lineup had now changed. Bayn was in the band, and we were no longer playing cover songs; we had written an album worth of origi-nals. We recorded them and were playing everywhere, promoting our music. Alcohol and getting high became my life. I started to think that the best inspiration to create music was birthed out of a mind-altered, drug-induced state. I would get high to write music and then get drunk to play it.

At different times in this period of my life, the voices of the past would haunt me. It was the voices of those who, at various times, tried to talk to me about God. Knowing God wasn't in favor of my lifestyle, nor the career choice I made, I didn't want to hear anything about Him. I continued down the staircase of madness that enveloped my life.

Our family had nothing really of religious background. My Uncle Jim was very active in his faith, and so was his family; outside of him, my aunts and uncles not so much. I think I only witnessed my Dad attend church a handful of times; he never talked to me about God, only that he existed.

I can still remember the times to this day, those distant voices coming from my childhood. Those messages of dying lost, fire, and brimstone, God's judgment on the world for their disobedience to Him, would visit me amid my worldly indulgences. The voice would come at the most obscure times. I would be at a club, surrounded by people, drinking and partying, and out of nowhere, the chilling reality would come to me; it was almost a paralyzing thought. *"Tom, these people don't know God, and if they were to die tonight, they would be lost, and if you were to die tonight, so would you.* I would have to shake myself and ask, *"Where did that come from? What kind of insane thought was that? Are you kidding yourself? This is what you've wanted your entire life."* I would shrug it off and try to block it out of my mind, but it would never altogether leave me. God was calling me, but I wasn't ready; I hadn't *"Hit Rock Bottom"* yet. Maybe this is where you're at? Perhaps you, a friend, or a loved one are in this place? Don't give up on them because God is dealing with them, and *"Rock Bottom"* hasn't come yet.

I had an experience one time when I was around eighteen. My cousins kept inviting me to go to church with them, so after their persistent harping, I said yes. At this point in life, I had shaved the sides of my head into a mohawk. I had pierced both of my ears and gotten a tattoo. Even though it was just to appease them, inside, I wanted to know God. This would be my first real encounter with God.

I got to church late. There were vacant seats in the foyer just beyond the sanctuary, so I sat down. I was alone, and what was about to happen was beyond anything I had anticipated. I listened to the message from the speakers overhead, and to this day, I can't tell you the title of that message or what it was about, but something the preacher had said from the Word of God touched me.

The preacher finished his homily; the assembly was now standing in their pews, getting ready for the altar call. I got up from where I was seated in the foyer to join my family in the sanctuary. As I rose from my seat, something inside of me felt strange. It was something I had never experienced before; God was drawing me to him. With the Spirit of God all over me, and this overwhelming conviction consuming me, I was starting to shake. As I opened those doors and crossed the threshold, the convicting power of God broke me, and I went to that altar and repented for my sins.

I began to weep as those memories from my childhood of being lost flooded my soul. The thought of my family being lost and the sinful life I was living broke my spirit. For the first time in my life, God really touched me and let me know He was real.

I was on cloud nine and felt clean for the first time in my life. I went home that day and told my friends that I was going to start going to church and make different choices for my life. I attended Bible study for a few weeks, but the world's influence and the love of my music choked the seed out. The calling of the world replaced the voice I heard that day in the foyer. Life returned to normal; the partying and playing guitar was back in full swing.

There's a saying I've heard many times throughout life that says, *"God moves in mysterious ways."* About a year after my first experience with God at that Church, Cary, a good friend of mine, invited me to go to church with him. Cary was in our musician's circle of friends and had recently started going to church. His life changed drastically. Cary cut all his long hair off; he abandoned his dreams of being a Rockstar and was now toting a Bible.

One night, Cary invited me to go to church, and I said yes. At this point, I was still practicing like crazy and living with my mom. Yet, internally there was still the small voice of God deep inside of me, reminding me that He touched me. I went to church that night, and this time, God not only touched me, but He filled me with His Spirit. This time I wasn't broken or repenting for sin or sobbing and shaking under conviction. It was a supernatural joy; there are no words to describe what it's like when God fills you with His Spirit.

I had now seen a different side of God. He wasn't just a God of wrath and judgment; I now knew that He was a God of joy and peace. It was unlike anything I had ever experienced before. I now realize that this was the beginning of the end. The dark road of addiction hadn't reached its peak, and the steps to hell were paved with gold waiting for me. I was going to be a Rockstar, and nothing was going to stop me.

The band grew in popularity, and so did the drinking and the insanity. By this time, I was twenty-one, and there was never a shortage of alcohol. On one particular occasion of debauchery, Pete called my place of employment. He told the secretary that he needed to speak to me because a dear friend of ours, Tony, had been in a horrible car accident and was being rushed to the hospital. After receiving such a horrifying message, I raced to the phone, only to hear laughter on the other end of the receiver when I said hello. I said, what's going on? Pete informed me that he made up that story to get me out of work so we could go drinking. Needless to say, I hung up the phone with a concerned look on my face and told them I would be heading to the hospital.

Life was going in a great direction, at least that's what I thought at the time. Our band was playing out regularly and promoting our own music. We had a great fan base, and drugs, alcohol, and girls were at center stage. Still, God dealt with me in the back of my mind and talked to me in subtle ways. Every now and then, I would have those thoughts come to me, saying, *"the wages of sin is death,"* and *"no man can serve two masters."* However, excessive drinking and partying had begun to erode our dedication to our dream and to each other. Members started skipping practice, and we were no longer the fine-tuned machine we once were. I can't tell you how it happened, but we finally parted ways. One of the original members would pass, another would move out of the country, and another would spend over a decade incarcerated. I joined another band that failed also. I was nearing rock bottom.

One night while my grandparents were over visiting, I overheard my sister April saying, to my grandma and mom, *"What is he going to do with his life? "He has nothing going for him; he's a loser."* It was true. I dropped out of high school, my band had failed, and I worked a dead-end job with no future. Her words were a cold slap in the face of reality.

I decided I was going to move out and show them. As life attacked me with its tsunami of responsibilities, I was forced to get a second job. My dreams were fading; I had no time to commit to a band nor practice my guitar. Life had become a meaningless cycle of mundane actions. My circle of friends was now gone since I moved; my life was empty. I was twenty-two years old and miserable, but God had His hand in all of it. I had finally *hit rock bottom, and I was ready to unplug.*

Drugs and Alcohol couldn't bring me the happiness they once did. For the first time in my young adult life, I experienced depression. In those dark hours, I would say to myself, *"If I had only listened to my Dad when I was in school and paid attention and got good grades, I might have had a career to fall back on."* But I didn't because no one could have told me that I would fail in being a Rockstar. I was lonely, a failure, and I had no future. I feared I would just become another high school statistical dropout. The majority of my high school friends had gone to college or joined the military. They were moving on with their lives, and there I was, stuck with no way out, living at rock bottom.

Cary had moved to the same town I had just moved to a few years prior. He had started going to a church there and was still on fire for God. I reached out to him to see if he wanted to get together. I wanted to talk about playing the guitar, and Cary wanted to talk about God. He reminded me about the experience we had as teenagers, the night God filled us both with His Spirit. This time I had more of a willingness to listen because of the loneliness of rock bottom. Cary would open up the Bible and ask me questions about God and my salvation, causing me to examine myself. (If you're witnessing to someone who may not be completely receptive, but you know God is dealing with them, please be patient and don't give up because it could be their salvation). I knew God was calling me, and He didn't want me living at *rock bottom,* and God doesn't want you living at *rock bottom* either.

Finally, the day came when I accepted Cary's offer to go to church with him. I was broken, ready for a change in my life. I was tired of always hitting a brick wall and never getting ahead. I didn't want to work two jobs for the rest of my life and live in a bedroom. I was ready to *unplug from rock bottom.* God was using all my failures to set up His glory in my life. *"Rock Bottom"* became the solid foundation on which I rebuilt my life. His ways are far exceeding beyond our ways, and I could have never seen it coming. *"For my thoughts are not your thoughts, neither are your ways my ways, saith the LORD. For as the heavens are higher than the earth, so are my ways higher than your ways and my thoughts than your thoughts"* **(Isaiah 55:8-9).** The divine orchestration was incredible.

In January of 1993, it would be the beginning of a new life that I'm still living today. I'll never forget what I wore to my first church service. I didn't have anything that resembled church attire. I wore cut-off sweat-pants, with long johns under them, a hoodie, and three-quarter length black leather boots to church that Sunday *(it's not about clothes, it's about the heart receiving the Word).* I'm sure by my external appearance, it was evident that I was a prime candidate for God. It was a fantastic service, unlike anything I had ever seen before. The church had a keyboard player, a drummer, a guitar player, a bass player, and the singing was heavenly, to say the least. Then the preacher got up and preached, unlike any other preacher I had ever heard. He preached, I don't know exactly, but I began to feel God pulling on my heartstrings; and His Spirit wanted to move in me. After the service ended that night, I said I wanted to come back next Sunday to church.

However, during the week after that Sunday service, I had gone out and used drugs, and the Lord convicted me about it. He showed me if I wanted to *unplug from rock bottom,* I had to submit to His Will. I de-cided I was done, and I wanted God more than getting high. I wanted

God more than being a Rockstar. I wanted God more than the person I wanted to be. I didn't want to be another statistical high school dropout.

The following Sunday, January 23rd, 1993, was the day my life changed for eternity. I went to church that night, and the preacher preached a message called, *"By Chance."* The message was about three characters in the bible named Naomi, Ruth, and Boaz. The preacher preached how God had divinely directed Ruth's steps to land on Boaz's field because she was supposed to be in the linage of Christ. The story also paralleled Naomi's struggles, the misfortunes, and woes she encountered in her journey back to God. That was my story of coming back to God and so many others.

That night after hearing the message about Naomi's return to God and Ruth's calling to God, I decided I would get baptized in Jesus' Name and take on his identity. I was a new creature in Christ, and the joy of the Lord became my strength. For the first time since the day God filled me with His Spirit years prior, I felt the joy I desperately longed for in my life. I *unplugged from rock bottom* and left a vacancy in the place where I once used to live. I was no longer feeling hopeless and discouraged about my life and its direction. I was encouraged because my life had meaning for the first time, and God was now leading me.

That was over twenty-five years ago, and I would be lying if I said I never had a low point in my walk with the Lord or that I have never failed Him. I've had both, but one thing I've never had, a *rock bottom,* like the place I used to live. This world is no longer my home; I'm just a stranger passing through on my journey. Today, I have a beautiful wife, three incredible children, and one granddaughter. I own my own home, have my own business, and I'm a blessed man. I'm not boasting about things or myself. My boast is only in the Lord and what He can do with anybody who decides to *unplug from rock bottom* and give Him a chance.

A certain man had two sons:_And the younger of them said to his father, "Father, give me the portion of goods that falleth to me."

— Luke 15:11

There's an old adage you have heard throughout life. *"The grass is greener on the other side of the fence."* It's simple but mighty. When it comes to human nature, trying to escape an unpleasant condition it may be facing, the deception of *"the grass looking greener on the other side of the fence"* comes calling.

Perhaps the best example of thinking the grass is greener on the other side of the fence is the Prodigals son's story in the gospel of Luke. In Luke's writings, you see the pilgrimage of a wayward son who has a longing for the unknown. He wants to see the other side of the fence! Unlike myself and so many others who tasted sin in excess, a generation has not; those who were born in the Father's house.

In my twenty-five years serving the Lord, I have seen this firsthand. Young people born and raised in the church have never tasted the world and its excess. They think the grass is greener on the other side of the "fence." They believe that there are no rules or restraints and that means freedom. I can remember when I left home, and I had that mentality. I had no one telling me what to do. No one telling me you can't go here, and you can't go there, etc.

In my personal opinion, I believe the prodigal son left the father's house way before he reached the age where it was an option. I believe his appetite for the world and the enticement of pleasure captured his heart. Like any good father, you can surmise he saw his son begin to drift towards the world. Without a doubt, he reached out to him. At first, the son may have been somewhat receptive to his father's warnings, but the longing for the unknown became a temptation that had swallowed him. A love for the world and what it had to offer was greater than any attempts made by his father. I imagine it got to the point where any efforts to stop his foolishness were met with hostility and aggression. Anger had now set in, and disdain for his parents and the rules of the house loathed him.

As they watched their son drift away, they felt helpless. The tipping point had reached its destination, and no longer could the curiosity be restrained; nothing could derail the inevitable.

Watching your child walk out the church doors and into the world's allure is heartbreaking. No one is promised tomorrow. As a parent, brother, or sister, you want to do everything in your power to stop the one you love from walking away from God. This is where you have to put your trust in the Lord. Thankfully, none of my children have left the Father's House, but I have friends whose children have left the church for the world. I have seen hearts bleed and souls torn to pieces over their children's backsliding. The best thing you can do as friends and parents of those who have left the church is, call on God. He's the only One who has all power in His Hand.

I graduated with honors from the school of hard knocks, and I never failed to make the dean's list. This is precisely what it takes for some to realize that it's not in the world. For those who have never tasted the sin of the world, it is a mysterious place. It doesn't appear horrendous from the outside looking in. High society paints a pretty glamorous portrait of it-self. They don't show you the misery, depression, and unhappiness because it's not what they thought it would be. All they show you is what they want to sell you. Reality and social media are two very different worlds.

The prodigal's eyes fell on the world and all its glitter. He was capti-vated by a "no restraint" lifestyle. All the things he had imagined while he was in his father's house, he was now doing. His appetites were being satisfied, and he wasted his money on riotous living. Sin is fun at first, but when the money is gone, so are the so-called friends.

And when he had spent all, there arose a mighty famine in that land; and he began to be in want.

And he went and joined himself to a citizen of that country; and he sent him into his fields to feed swine.

And he would fain have filled his belly with the husks that the swine did eat: and no man gave unto him.

– Luke 15:14-16

This world will use you up and throw you away; you're disposable. Everybody is your "friend" as long as they have something to gain from you. There are countless stories about the lives of people who once had money and fame that ran parallel with the prodigal's son. When the money was gone, so were the friends. Penniless, hungry, broken, and all alone with no one who cared about him and lucky to be alive, the Prodigal *"Hit Rock Bottom."*

It was devastating to watch their son leave home, not knowing what his life would become. I genuinely believe some people love God, yet they still leave the father's house for various reasons. Hurts, caused by those in the church. Hurts are caused by their parents or siblings. Self-condemnation for sin, or sometimes it's merely to find out what's on "the other side of the fence."

God still loves them and doesn't want them to be lost. When His attempts with the Word are not met with receptivity, He allows them to detour off the straight and narrow. God is longsuffering, gentle, and He's all-knowing. It's just going to take some time before they *hit rock bottom and unplug!*

The loneliness, feeling destitute, and sinking deeper and deeper into a life of utter depravity was the prodigal son's *"Rock Bottom!"* Don't give up on your loved one; it's not over. I believe the moment is about to come. The revelation of the grass wasn't greener on the other side! Right now, you've got a loved one that is just about ready to come home; they're nearing their bottom. The day is coming sooner than you think. Their approaching and ready to *"Hit Rock Bottom and Unplug."* It was the prayer of his parents and friends, and it will be your prayers that bring them home. You know it pained his mother and father to watch their son walk away from what was right (God), for what was wrong (the world), as it would you, but it had to be that way, so, in the end, he would be saved.

"Prodigal's Son," a metaphor for those born and raised in the house of God, then leave for the world. The allurement of pleasures, and the pseudo image of life, like one big party with no rules or restraint, captivate their hearts and sweep them away. The reality of their wrong decisions won't come until they finally *"Hit Rock Bottom."* Sadly, many who *"Hit Rock Bottom"* have nothing to fall back on because they don't have God in their life, but fortunately, the Prodigal had God.

His parents planted enough of the Word into his heart as a child. Growing up and attending Sunday School, coupled with their love, would be the very thing that would bring him home. This was the best thing that could have happened to him. You never want to see a child or a relative walk away from God and go to the world. But, sometimes, it takes them seeing the other side of the fence to realize it's not what they thought it would be. There are young people I love and watched grow up in the church, walk away from the Father's house, and I believe they will be back. I'm going to keep on loving them until they return, and so should you. The Lord told us, *"I will never leave thee, nor forsake thee,"* we should do the same for one another. The day will come for them like it did the prodigal when they *"Hit Rock Bottom"* and come home.

> *And when he came to himself, he said, "How many hired servants of my father's have bread enough and to spare, and I perish with hunger!*
> *I will arise and go to my father, and will say unto him, Father, I have sinned against heaven, and before thee."*

— Luke 15:17-18

The Prodigal, he had to face himself, and so does every person who walks away from God, wanting to come back. This, itself self is such a huge mountain to climb for a myriad of reasons. For some, there are new friends, and relationships that will have to be severed. For others, they will have to face the people they used as their excuse to leave in the first place. Probably one of the biggest detours of all is self-condemnation. Knowing you let others down, and most of all, you let God down. But, in the Apostle John's writing, he pen's the rebuttal to self-condemnation, *"For if our heart condemns us, God is greater than our heart, and knoweth all things."* God knows the beginning from the end, just as God watched the son walk away. He knew one day the son would also come home. God is greater than backsliding.

> *And he arose, and came to his father. But when he was*
> *yet a great way off, his father saw him, and had compassion,*
> *and ran, and fell on his neck, and kissed him.*
>
> *— Luke 15:20*

The love of God never fails, and He will always embrace a repenting son/daughter who has gone astray and decides to come home! Like the prodigal, others, and myself, sometimes you have to take a journey to a far country. Not necessarily physically, but mentally. You can be going to church, sitting in the house of God, and be in a far country. You haven't left because you're enticed by the allurement of the world; you're just burned out from the struggles of life. That's okay; you're not alone. God knows, sees, and understands where you're at and how you got there. He knows you're going to come home.

The moment will come when you least expect it. It may be while the preacher is preaching that God touches you. It may be while somebody is testifying in the church, and you're moved by the Spirit of God. Alone in thought, prayer, or reading the Word may be when you come to yourself. You realize you are in a pit of despair, you've been dining with the swine, and you want out. You have to battle the condemnation that wants to keep you trapped in the cell of separation—the guilt, and shame, and the humiliation of facing those you've let down. *"Unplug"* from those feelings.

I've made some pretty drastic mistakes in my life and left the Father's house spiritually speaking. It didn't take long, and I found myself in a pit, and I knew there was only one way out. I had to turn from the place I was at and head in the direction of home. Like the Prodigal, myself, and many others, you realized you didn't ever want to end up at the place of "rock bottom" again when you come to yourself. Whatever it was that brought you to that point, you have decided to *"Unplug"* permanently from it. God has so miraculously brought you out, and now you've started your journey home.

The book of Psalms says, *"if I make my bed in hell, behold thou are there."* Hell is used figuratively, and it represents *"Rock Bottom."* The Psalmist depicts the faithfulness and love of God to those who *"Hit Rock Bottom,"* letting us know God has not left us, but He's right there. We've all had low points at different times, and for some, its prison addictions, and for others, it's just drifting away while sitting in the pew. No matter how deep of a hole you find yourself in, God is right there. His arm is stretched out and ready to bring you home. It may not be easy, and depending on how deep your pit is, it may take a while. However, the minute you *unplug,* our God will bring you out. Take the challenge, unplug, and walk away from rock bottom, never to return again! God's waiting for you!

CHAPTER 4

NEVER JUDGE A BOOK BY ITS COVER BECAUSE YOU HAVEN'T READ THE PAGES IN BETWEEN!

Statistics have said, the average person's attention span is approximately eighty-sixed seconds. Snapchat, and other social apps, have dumbed down our focus to ten to twenty-second videos. We live in a world of the here and now. This is the 21st century or the information age. The world has crossed a new threshold and quickly closed the door behind it. Values that once were the standard are now considered the extreme right and are not conducive to modern-day theology. This generation is quickly turned off or turned on by snippets of news briefs that are the hot buttons that fuel their self-absorbed, selfish world.

I have come to know and believe, not everything can be adequately judged in a *"Snap"* or a *"Tweet."* We cannot judge everything at face value. Everybody has a story. Character, personality, habits, and appearances all have foundations. It's not until we unearth the external layers do we begin to understand and clearly see the basis for their actions.

Probably some of my favorite reading is in the Old Testament. I love 1st and 2nd Kings and 1st and 2nd Chronicles. The history and culture are so rich. Within those books, the life-and-death of King Manasseh is recorded. Manasseh has been revered by many as one of the most nefarious Kings of Judah. Manasseh's introduction is less than stellar; the bible says, *"He did that which was evil in the sight of the Lord" (2 Kings 21:2).* This sets the tone for events that would unravel in his life and decisions that would haunt him to his grave.

Manasseh's ascent to the throne wasn't because his father, Hezekiah, had grown old, and he had reached the age of maturity and was ready to embrace the scepter of Kingship. No, that wasn't the case at all; it was because his father had passed, and it was his responsibility to take the throne.

During the process of writing this book, my father passed rather suddenly. He was diagnosed with cancer at the end of December 2017 and died on February 1st, 2018. He will never get a chance to read it, and this chapter especially has become more personal to me through this journey of *"Unplugging"* because he played a massive part in it.

Though I got to enjoy forty-seven years of my father, to me, it still wasn't long enough. Every morning when I sit down to write, I have a poster board full of my father's pictures. There are photos of him with all my children at various ages of their lives. My youngest daughter (Faith), and her husband (Judah), had their first child. Sadly, he will never get to experience the joy of becoming a great-grandfather. My heart is broken for my youngest sister (Ashley); she and her husband have just had their first child. Our father only got to hold my niece one time before he passed. Grief is real, and the loss of a parent is one of the hardest things a person can go through. Some handle it better than others, and so the narrative begins with Manasseh.

> *Manasseh was twelve years old when he began to reign,*
> *and reigned fifty and five years in Jerusalem. And he did that*
> *which was evil in the sight of the LORD, after the abomi-*
> *nations of the heathen, whom the LORD cast out before the*

children of Israel. For he built up again the high places which
Hezekiah his father had destroyed; and he reared up altars
for Baal, and made a grove, as did Ahab king of Israel; and
worshipped all the host of heaven, and served them.

– 2 Kings 21:1-3

I can't help but ask the question, why? Why did Manasseh go in the complete opposite direction of his father, Hezekiah? Why did he destroy what made his father's legacy so great? His father, Hezekiah's devotion to the Lord God of Israel, was rivaled by no one, save King David. When you read about Hezekiah and his introduction into the Bible, you find that it was during spiritual apostasy. Israel had fallen back into idol worship, and the favor of God was no longer theirs. Restless with the fact that he and the children of Israel were living below their means, it was time for a change. Hezekiah turned the tide; he was a spiritual revolutionist. Hezekiah came out of the corner, swinging at the young age of twenty-five. He was on fire for God and wanted all of God for himself and the nation he was King over. This is a metaphor for what this challenge is about. It starts with you tearing down the things that cause you to live below your natural and spiritual means.

Hezekiah removed the high places, and brake the images,
and cut down the groves, and brake in pieces the brasen ser-
pent that Moses had made: for unto those days the children
of Israel did burn incense to it: and he called it Nehushtan.
He trusted in the LORD God of Israel; so that after him was
none like him among all the kings of Judah, nor any that
were before him For he clave to the LORD, and departed not
from following him, but kept his commandments, which the
LORD commanded Moses And the LORD was with him;
and he prospered whithersoever he went forth.

So why did Manasseh go astray when he had such a Godly heritage? His great, great, great grandfather was the sweet psalmist, King David, arguably the greatest King of Judah that ever lived. They never had money struggles; he had the best of the best. After all, he was born into royalty. I'm sure most people would have traded places with him in a heartbeat and never commit the atrocities he did. You might look at Manasseh and say to yourself, *"Manasseh never really wanted to serve the Lord; that's why he went to the world"*?

How many times have you *judged a book by its cover* without ever reading the pages in between? Have you ever had your life judged by its cover or seen people *judge a book by its cover* without ever reading what's written on the pages in between?

Maybe that's one of the problems with so many people in the world and in the church. They look at a person on the street, or when they walk in the church, their clothes are less than fashionable; they scorn and make fun of them. I have witnessed both, it's so hypocritical, and God hates it.

All too often, people never stop to read the pages in between; they simply arrive at their own conclusions based on external observation. They rarely ever delve into the internal affairs that propel their actions or appearance. I have come to the realization that every book cover has a story. Within those pages, every life has a backdrop to its setting, and most people are in critical condition spiritually and require emergency surgery—their trauma patients. The Church is the Spiritual I.C.U.

GRIEF AT A YOUNG AGE

I believe that for Manasseh and others, rebellion is birthed out of anger and hurt from losing a parent. My sister Ivonne shared with me she has had to battle anger, and I have to admit, I've had to fight anger at my dad. His death could have been avoided if he had gone to the doctor when he first started showing signs that there was a problem instead of ignoring it. The rebellion was Manasseh's outlet to vent his pain. The emotions, the thought process, and confusion of his world turned upside down left him in a tailspin. Manasseh was in critical condition; he was a trauma patient. Whenever you lose a family member, grief can affect you in many ways.

Laura recently attended a support group for "grief." She shared with me some of the stories of those hurting. Grief is real, and it's excruciating. People in God or out of God are hurting and have dealt with pain throughout their lives. Some were physically and sexually abused as children; others had spousal abuse. Grief has many forms.

Laura and I lost a child at birth; it's one of the hardest things a parent can go through, especially the mother. For nine months, Laura felt the kicking and turning and all the emotions that come with pregnancy. After our daughter passed, Laura battled depression, anger, and a whirlwind of emotions. Those emotions would take years to overcome and to finally have peace with her passing. We visit her grave on her birthday, and it's a resurfacing of that horrible day, but God has given us comfort knowing we'll see her again.

Three years before Manasseh was born, his father, Hezekiah, had fallen sick and was at the point of death. The Lord sent Isaiah the prophet to King Hezekiah with a message, *"Thus saith the LORD, Set thine house in order; for thou shalt die, and not live" (2Kings 20:1).* Then without another word, Isaiah turned and walked away.

After hearing such a scathing rebuke, one would think those were some pretty harsh words from God. But, Hezekiah was not just any man; this was the man that restored Judah to a relationship with the Lord. Hezekiah destroyed anything and everything contrary to God! Hezekiah tore down the altars of Baal; he destroyed the high places. Hezekiah was a man that trusted in the Lord God of Israel for everything, and now he had just been given a death sentence from God. Sometimes things just don't make sense in your mind, how God moves and speaks.

Then he (Hezekiah) turned his face to the wall, and prayed unto the LORD, saying, "I beseech thee, O LORD, remember now how I have walked before thee in truth and with a perfect heart, and have done that which is good in thy sight. And Hezekiah wept sore" (2 Kings 20:3). While some might get angry, others might wallow in self-pity and say, *"this is what I get for living for God and doing his will!"* Hezekiah's response was the complete opposite. His character, and love for the Lord God of Israel, exceeded his diagnosis. While Isaiah was going out into the middle court, God spoke to him again and said,

> *"Turn again, and tell Hezekiah the captain of my people, Thus saith the LORD, the God of David thy father, I have heard thy prayer, I have seen thy tears: behold, I will heal thee: on the third-day thou shalt go up unto the house of the LORD." "And I will add unto thy days fifteen years."*
> *– 2 Kings 20:5-6*

So, it was in the final years of Hezekiah's life, Manasseh was born unto him. Manasseh undoubtedly was his pride and joy, and heir to the throne, Manasseh would be king. Hezekiah's celebrations were only short-lived because he would never see past his son's twelfth year. You can imagine Manasseh standing at his father's funeral. He couldn't believe his father was gone. As the sea of people passed the casket paying their final respects, the sounds of weeping could be heard in the background; he was numb.

RAGE OUT OF CONTROL

Manasseh's ascent to the throne paled in comparison to the pain of his father's passing; his heart had been ripped out by his father's death. A father, who no doubt was the love and adoration of his life. When anger is fueled with unbearable pain, the carnage can become unthinkable, and the grief is indescribable. At times, the mind can't cope with what it's going through, and actions become dictated by emotions, unharnessed. Try to imagine yourself in his shoes, or maybe you've been there and know his pain?

"Rage out of control" would be the best way to describe the actions that followed Manasseh and his anger. I have personally seen in my life and others' lives how anger can be fueled by the hurts caused by those you love. These are some of the most challenging injuries to *"unplug"* from. So often, you are judged by *"the cover, and not the pages in-between."* People can quickly assert judgment and start casting stones with their words, and their harsh criticisms only fuel the rage even more. And yet, they don't know or understand the reason behind the actions.

> *Manasseh built up again the high places which Hezekiah his father had destroyed; and he reared up altars for Baal, and made a grove, and worshipped all the host of heaven, and served them. And he built altars in the house of the LORD, of which the LORD said, In Jerusalem will I put my name. And he built altars for all the host of heaven in the two courts of the house of the LORD. And he made his son pass through the fire, and observed times, and used enchantments, and dealt with familiar spirits and wizards: he wrought much wickedness in the sight of the LORD, to provoke him to anger. And he set a graven image of the grove that he had made in the house, of which the LORD said to David, and to Solomon his son, In this house, and in Jerusalem, which I have chosen out of all tribes of Israel, will I put my name for ever:*
>
> *– 2 Kings 21:3-7*

As if all that wasn't enough, what you are about to read is unthinkable, inconceivable, and unimaginable, that as a parent, I'm lost for words. Knowing the love I have for my children and what they mean to me, where Manasseh's mind took him to commit such an atrocity of wickedness, it is mind-boggling. It only shows us what pain can cause you to do.

> *And he made his son pass through the fire, and observed times, and used enchantments, and dealt with familiar spirits and wizards: he wrought much wickedness in the sight of the LORD, to provoke him to anger.*
>
> *– 2 Kings 21:6*

I want to take a second and draw your attention to what it means, too, *"making his son pass through the fire."* Making a child pass through the fire was the practice of human sacrifice to the heathen god Molech. Molech's image was a human figure with a bull's head and outstretched arms, ready to receive the children destined for sacrifice. The image was made and shaped out of metal and was heated red hot by a fire kindled within. The children were laid on Molech's arms, and then they rolled off into the fiery pit below. To drown the cries of the victims, flutes were played, and drums were beaten. History says mothers stood by without tears or sobs to give the impression of their voluntary character of the offering. This is something you, or I, could never imagine, yet Manasseh did this to his son.

History also says that Manasseh killed the prophet Isaiah and had him "sawn-asunder" (cut in half). As I was reading Isaiah's account of him coming to Hezekiah on his sickbed and pronouncing his death sentence, I wonder if somehow Manasseh blamed Isaiah for his father's passing? Maybe Isaiah was one of the prophets God sent to him to stop his insanity, and he killed him because he preached against his sin? Manasseh rebuilt all the things that his father had once destroyed. He destroyed everything that made his father a great leader, which brought God's favor to Israel. Could it be because of the anger that he felt about his father's loss that propelled his actions? I have the proclivity to think so. I've listed below an outline of Manasseh's rebellious actions. I want you to read it and ask yourself, how would you judge him?

Damage Survey

- He built up again the "high places" – a place of false worship
- He reared up "altars for Baal'" – a pagan god
- He made "a groove" – an alternate place of worship other than the temple
- He worshipped "the stars and the heavens."
- He placed "altars" for the host of heaven in the house of God – defiled the temple
- Offered his son a living human sacrifice to a pagan god – an abomination
- He observed times, enchantments, dealt with familiar spirits – witchcraft
- Seducing the children of Israel to sin worse than the heathen – caused his fellow brothers and sisters to sin against God, worse than those who don't know God.
- Murdered so many innocent people till he filled the city of God with blood from one end to the other!

If you didn't know his life's history, how would you *"judge the book by its cover?"* According to Moses Law, on every account, he should have been punished by the death penalty. Would that be your sentence?

One might find it hard to believe that God loved such a wicked King like Manasseh, who may have killed His prophet, and you know for sure killed innocent people. Yet, God did not kill him or depose him from his throne. Instead, God allowed Manasseh to live, and not only did He let him live, but Manasseh had the longest reign out of any King in Judah or Israel. Why would God allow such an evil man not only to live but have the longest reign out of any King in the history of Israel's monarch?

> *"The LORD seeth not as man seeth; for man looketh on the outward appearance, but the LORD looketh on the heart."*
>
> — *1 Samuel 16:7*

THE HARVEST

> *"Be not deceived; God is not mocked: for whatsoever a man soweth, that shall he also reap."*
>
> — *Galatians 6:7*

> *And the LORD spake to Manasseh, and to his people: but they would not hearken.*
> *Wherefore the LORD brought upon them the captains of the host of the king of Assyria, which took Manasseh among the thorns, and bound him with fetters, and carried him to Babylon.*
>
> — *2 Chronicles 33:10-11*

The time had come, and the judgment seat of God wrapped its gavel on the desk. The sentence was handed down, the verdict read "GUILTY ON ALL ACCOUNTS." The decision's execution was implemented; *"Bound with fetters, and carried off to Babylon, Manasseh was in affliction!"* Now the roles had reversed, and no longer was Manasseh, the predator, but he was now the prey. No longer was he the afflicter; he was now the afflicted. Transported to Babylon, bound in chains and fettered, Manasseh had no way of escape.

It was a long road to Babylon, where he knew a prison cell would be waiting for him or possibly even death. Manasseh would have time to think about his life, choices, decisions, and captivity. For some, like Manasseh, it may take a prison cell to *unplug* from the pain. Unlike God, man would have probably left Manasseh in prison, restricted to solitary confinement for the rest of his life, and never giving him a chance for parole. Man is so quick to *judge a book/a person's life by its cover* without *ever reading the pages in-between.*

I want to share an experience with you that I encountered that took me aback. It made me rethink how I look at people, and it changed my life in a way I'll try to describe on the following pages. Our company services a good portion of our lower state. I average between forty-five to fifty thousand miles a year in travel. Sometimes, I have to commute through the impoverished areas of the inner-city. I'll see a homeless person, drug dealer, streetwalkers, panhandlers, and winos on any given day. An overwhelming spirit of humility and thankfulness overtakes me because, if God had not intervened in my life, that could have been me. I will never forget the time I was in the heart of Detroit leaving a home I had just inspected; I had just pulled up to a stoplight and as I turned to my right, there, standing at the intersection, was a streetwalker. She was clad in next to nothing for clothes. Our eyes made contact, and as I looked into her deep brown eyes, I saw a life of pain, sorrow, and survival. Even though it was only a moment or two, it seemed like minutes passed as we made eye contact.

The light changed, and I drove away, changed forever. Instead of looking at her with disdain, I felt compassion and remorse for her. Given a choice, I don't think she would have chosen her current profession --she had to survive the best way she knew how to. She was somebody's daughter. Where were her parents? Did she have siblings or children? If she could tell you her story, I don't think you would be so quick to judge her so harshly. Was she abused sexually or physically as a child? Was she a runaway trying to find some means of survival on the streets, and this was the only way she knew how to? Undoubtedly, she was tough as brass.

One cannot survive on Detroit's streets, especially in her profession, without becoming calloused from expressing outward emotions. How many times had she been beaten and assaulted by a client and left for dead? And yet, with no way of escape, she returns to the streets for survival. I would imagine she wanted a better life, but she was trapped. Even though our encounter was at a traffic light for a few seconds, I could tell by her countenance, she expressed *anger and pain*. Undoubtedly, she doesn't remember me or our encounter, but I'll never forget her and how she changed my life.

You've heard throughout life that people say "they" have "anger Issues," so you try to avoid that person because no one likes being around an angry, miserable person. To a degree, society has some *anger issues;* look at all the road rage stories you read in the news. Sadly, because most of our society doesn't have the Lord in their life and His Word, they have no Spiritual governor over their emotions to help control them. Even having His Word, sometimes humanity can get the best of you.

As I'm sitting here writing, a wave of emotions (the author's confession) has just enveloped me about my own *"anger issues"* that stemmed from my childhood with my father. As a child, I hated my dad growing up, and as soon as I could leave home at the legal age of seventeen, I did.

My father and I didn't have the best of relationships growing up. By the time I was a teenager, he was going through his second divorce. I was by no means a perfect child; I had rebellion working inside of me. My dad would always say to me growing up, *"I can make a hundred more just like you,"* which only fueled my hatred towards him. My dad never beat me physically but verbally; he would be very condescending. At times he was very oppressive and would say to me, *"I don't care what you want, it's my way, and that's the only way."* These words would only cement the seeds of anger deeper in my heart.

Now that he has passed, I regret holding those things against him and not forgiving him. My dad made several attempts to say he was sorry and correct his wrongs. I forgave him, but I kept my walls up and wouldn't let him in because of my resentments. He loved my children dearly, was a wonderful grandfather to them, and would do anything for them. If they had a science or math question, they would call him, and he would love to give them the answer to help them. It made me happy to see them have a good relationship with him, but I still harbored the *anger issues* that now haunt me. As I walked out of his hospital room the night he passed, a tsunami of guilt drowned me. I would never have a chance to have the relationship I always wanted because the door had just closed. The times he reached out to me to rebuild the relationship afresh was now gone because of the roadblock I had built. As I hugged his lifeless body, I said, I love you, Dad. My heart wrenched, and I experienced a pain second to none. He was gone and never to return. If only I would have let go and accepted his repentance like a "Christian" is supposed to, I would not have had to live with this guilt. I never had *unplugged* from my anger. But, instead, I wanted him to feel how I felt as a child. It was so stupid and selfish that I wanted him to suffer like he made me. I was such a fool.

I still can remember our last conversation. I was standing next to his bed, reflecting on the good times of my childhood, and there were plenty when it was just he and I. It was brief. He had come back to consciousness momentarily, and his last words to me were, *"yeah, we had some good times."* I told him I loved him, and he said, *"I love you too, son,"* and those were his last words to me. As tears stream down my face, I have to pause because my vision is blurred, and I'm sobbing very heavily. I've finally *unplugged* from my childhood anger; only now it's too late. The price was very great. I never really got a chance to *read the pages in between the cover of my father's life* because he never shared very much of it with me.

Looking at the childhood pictures of him on the collages, each of them telling a story. There were many photos I had never seen before, revealing my dad as a little boy laughing and having fun. Never did that little boy in those pictures ever think his life would end with cancer at the age of sixty-four. I learned a lot about my dad from those who shared the stories behind the photos of him. Stories of childhood adventures and his teenage recklessness were expounded on. Pictures giving insight into a part of his world I had never known. I miss him more than words can describe and writing this has been healing for me. My daughter Faith made him a photo collage of our family while he was in the hospital to look at, and that collage now hangs above my desk. Every morning I look at his photos when I sit down to write, and I want to tell him I'm sorry, but I can't; he's gone. I want to tell him I love him, but I can't; he's gone. King Solomon summed up anger like this, *"anger resteth in the bosom of fools" (Ecclesiastes 7:9).*

For the first time in your life, *unplug* from your anger and realize it's got you in a prison cell, bound with chains and fetters! Holding onto it only hurts you. Yes, you may have lashed out at those who had hurt you to make them feel the way you did, but in reality, you're still suffering because of them. Stop letting their wrongs be yours. Share with somebody your pain, go to therapy, and get counsel from a spiritual leader.

I was a fool, and anger rested in my soul for many years against my father. As a child, I was too young to understand and unable to comprehend his life and ours. I made it my mission statement as a father to never be like my dad. I have shared my childhood with them to try and help them understand where I came from and my shortcomings.

> *For whom the Lord loveth he chasteneth, and scourgeth every son whom he receiveth."*
>
> *– Heb 12:6*

As a child, or as an adult living for God, you are His children, and when your ways do not please Him and you go astray, He will correct you.

The imprisonment of Manasseh was the love and mercy of an Almighty God. God knows and understands His creation better than those that are so quick to judge it. Looking at Manasseh's life at this point, one might think to themselves, *"I knew it, it was just a matter of time, I knew God would get him,"* but not how you think. God understood what really kindled all the hate inside Manasseh that stemmed from the pain he felt from his father's loss. God knows your pain and what fuels it. I believe that was why God never removed him from his Kingship or took his life.

I'm not advocating nor insinuating because you have a terrible childhood, it gives you a right to commit atrocities towards people. Manasseh rightfully deserved to go to prison for life or receive the death penalty for his crimes against humanity. Prison is a punishment of time and thought. Manasseh had a lot of time to think about what he did, and so do you.

Maybe your prison cell is where you'll find yourself, acknowledging the things you've done, and take ownership instead of victimhood? Your life may appear to be a bed of roses, but inwardly it's a bier patch full of thorns and thistles, and hostile judgments cast at others *(like Manasseh, whom you've judged),* and yet you've never read the pages in between.

In reality, those judgments mask your own insecurities that stem from your past. Maybe it takes a prison cell to find yourself to *unplug.* *"Reading the pages in between the cover"* will help you better understand where those who you judge are coming from. Instead of being so quick to play judge, jury, and executioner to those who offend you, take the time to *read the pages in-between.* I bet if you did, you'd have a better understanding of who they really are and where they're coming from, and you'd have more mercy in your own life.

God is the one who judges the heart more than the actions when it comes to His people. Howbeit, the two are directly connected. It's the heart God will use to change the actions through His Word and Spirit. Let God be God, and just because the harvest someone receives isn't what you think they should, does not mean it isn't what God believes they deserve!

Take, for example, the woman taken in adultery in the Gospel of John chapter 8. There were some issues in her life that led her to commit such a sin. Her accusers, the self-righteous Scribes and Pharisees, sought the death penalty by stoning. But Jesus' answer was not so, *"He that is without sin among you, let him first cast a stone at her."* Jesus took it one step further to show His love and mercy, for sins birthed from wounds and issues of the heart. *"Woman, where are those thine accusers? hath no man condemned thee?"* She said, No man, Lord. *"Neither do I condemn thee: go, and sin no more" (John 8:10-11).*

God is not so quick to condemn like we condemn. God *doesn't judge a book by its cover* because He's read the pages in between. Manasseh's story doesn't end in a prison cell, and neither does yours. Your greatness lies just outside of the doors, along with your freedom. Manasseh couldn't undo the past, and neither can you. But, he changed his future by *unplugging* from it, and so will you.

CHAPTER 5

UNPLUGGING FROM YOUR PAST

The title for chapter 5 came to me while driving to work one day, *"Unplugging from Your Past."* That morning I had an excellent conversation with my brother-in-law, Joe. We talked about staying motivated to work out, dieting, and maintaining our focus on wellness. During our discussion, he shared with me that every morning we face two things in the mirror: our *weakness* and our *strength,* and it's up to us to decide which one will prevail. I began to dwell on that after we ended our conversation, and the Lord expanded on that thought and showed me that there are actually three faces we look at in the mirror every morning.

THE THREE FACES IN THE MIRROR

The Past. It's the culmination of choices and the decisions and their outcomes, both good and bad. This is neither profound nor abstract; it's just the truth you must face every day in the mirror. Your past doesn't define you. You can change who you are at this moment. Don't let your past be a stumbling block but a steppingstone. Let it become the inspiration to move you forward, with the tenacity and intent of never going back.

The Present. Even though you may not have the ability to control every aspect of the "Present," it is subjective. Making the right choices can lead you to be victorious today.

The Future. It's the door of opportunity that is waiting for you to open tomorrow. The Future is unknown and can be intimidating and thrilling at the same time. *"Eye hath not seen, nor ear heard, neither have entered into the heart of man, the things which God hath prepared for them that love him."-. 1 Cor 2:9*

Every morning consciously or subconsciously, you face all three in the mirror. The face that you choose to rule in the mirror will be the victor of the day. The definition of the word *"Past"* means *"having existed or taken place in a period before the present."*

You can't undo history or rewrite the past. The longer you try to, the longer you'll live in yesterday's regrets, and the longer you're going to live without the victory of today and tomorrow.

One of the keys to unplugging from your past is confronting it. Most people do not like confrontation, but sometimes it's unavoidable. Not only did Manasseh have to confront his past, but he also had to confront God. *When he was in affliction, he besought the LORD his God, and humbled himself greatly before the God of his fathers (2 Chronicles 33:12).*

To be humble is a reflection and expression offered in the spirit of submission. The Bible doesn't tell us how long he was in prison, but one thing about jail, it's a place of reflecting. I believe Manasseh took a fearless and moral inventory of his life and assessed his actions without partiality. He became brutally honest with himself and with God as he looked in the mirror of life, as he faced all three.

His pedigree was deplorable, and in his prison cell, Manasseh found himself, weighed in the balances on the scales of justice. His rage had catapulted him to levels beyond comprehension, crossing spiritual lines unlike anything ever seen in the history of Israel. I believe this was the turning point in his life.

THE PAST

As Manasseh began to reflect, I can only imagine the visual imagery that played over and over in his mind. Remembering the look of horror on his son's face as he offered him as a human sacrifice. An image etched so deep into his heart and mind, it would haunt him to his grave—the death of Isaiah, the prophet, whom he had ordered to be sawn asunder, and the countless lives that were killed in his sanguinary quest.

If there ever was a man that could allow his past to condemn him, it would be Manasseh. His crimes are written in black and white for the whole world to see. Because his actions happened thousands of years ago, they are not as impactful. However, if you were to replace Manasseh's name with the likes of *Adolf Hitler, Joseph Stalin,* or *Saddam Hussein,* you are instantly grounded to the sinisterness of his crimes. Would you grant them clemency?

THE PRESENT

The *"Present."* The point between the *"Past"* and *"Future"* is it's the middle face you look at in the mirror of decision every morning. To the left, you possibly see the face of the past, a visage of sorrow. An unhealthy codependent lifestyle of abuse that you've become accustomed to—a corridor of misery where the pangs impale your life, and those portraits decorate the walls. To the right is the uncertainty of the future. This is where Manasseh stood, and so do you.

One of the first things you learned in Alcoholics Anonymous is taking responsibility for your actions. You have to admit that you were powerless to the vices that had you bound. For the first time in his life, Manasseh had to take ownership of his actions and realized that he was powerless without God.

You might be asking yourself, how do you know Manasseh took ownership of his actions and repented? Because of what his great, great Uncle

Solomon penned on parchment for the world to read. It's a declaration of what God will do when you take ownership of your actions. *"If my people, which are called by my name, shall humble themselves, and pray, and seek my face, and turn from their wicked ways; then will I hear from heaven and will forgive their sin. Now mine eyes shall be open, and mine ears attend unto the prayer that is made"* (2 Chronicles 7:14-15).

I'm almost certain this is where Manasseh's healing and restoration began, and so will yours. I can remember that moment in my life; I remember kneeling down and humbling myself to God and what I said, this is the turning point in your life and the beginning of your deliverance from the past.

"Where do I begin? What do I say? How do I say it? All the things I've done wrong, can I be forgiven?" These were the thoughts that went through my mind as I humbled myself to God. Did God really love me like I heard when I was a little boy, the few times I had gone to Sunday school with the lady from across the street? Could God really love and forgive me? Would God really pardon all my wrongs, and the wickedness, of my *past*? I had never really prayed, and to be honest, I didn't know how to. I just got real with God. I told Him I'm sorry, and I wanted to change from who I was to what He wanted me to be, and so did Manasseh.

I haven't been able to find in the Bible or any other book, Manasseh's prayer. However, his humble sincerity with the Lord was so impactful that it moved God to bring him out of his prison. If you want out of your prison, the best place to start is humility and sincerity with the Lord in prayer. Maybe, his great grandfather, King David, whom the bible says, *"was a man after God's own heart,"* is where he drew his inspiration to pray from? I believe Manasseh reached back into the recesses of his mind and attempted to recite Psalm 51. It was David's prayer when he found himself in a similar place in life like Manasseh. David had failed God miserably, and it appeared like there was no hope. All Manasseh could remember were just bits and pieces of it; his prayer possibly went something like this.

"Have mercy upon me, O God, according to thy loving-kindness: according unto the multitude of thy tender mercies blot out my transgressions....Wash me thoroughly from mine iniquity, and cleanse me from my sin....For I acknowledge my transgressions: and my sin is ever before me....Against thee, thee only, have I sinned, and done this evil in thy sight: that thou mightest be justified when thou speakest, and be clear when thou judgest....Create in me a clean heart, O God; and renew a right spirit within me....Deliver me from bloodguiltiness, O God, thou God of my salvation: and my tongue shall sing aloud of thy righteousness"

You can find yourself trapped in the prison of your mind, haunted and tormented, with the guilt from your past. The carnal mind taunts and convinces you that the damage is so severe and so catastrophic, there is no way you can ever recover. The hurts and pain you've inflicted on others are beyond salvation. You can't be forgiven. Wrong!

Manasseh's life, and the paralyzing atrocities he willfully committed against God and the children of God, one would wonder, how can someone like that be forgiven? Could God really understand that Manasseh's actions were fueled by hurts from his childhood?

God can really forgive the p*ast,* so you can have a future. Yes, He can. All the things Manasseh did and what he had to face in that solitary cell of emptiness, God knew. The defeat, the despair, and the overwhelming guilt of his own pain, God knew also. God knows the beginning from the end, and you're the one who writes the pages in between. In your plight of despair like Manasseh, you can find the faith to believe God knows where you're at.

Prayer, with sincere repentance, God will not deny, nor will He reject. God will unequivocally grant you complete forgiveness and *unplug you from your past.*

We have a magnet of *"The Serenity Prayer"* on our fridge because of Laura's program background. I feel it is very applicable when facing the guilt from your past. It's here where you start a new beginning, and when you apply its principles, your past will no longer control your future.

> *Grant Me, The Serenity To, Accept The Things I Can't Change*
> *The Courage To Change The Things I Can, And*
> *The Wisdom To Know The Difference.*

You can't change the *"Past,"* but God can give you the ability to accept it. God will provide you with the courage to change the things you can in the *present,* and the wisdom to know the difference is the beginning of a new *future.*

"UNPLUGGING" FROM THE PAST AND BUILDING A NEW FUTURE

Truth be told, countless lives have risen from the depth of despair and into the blazing lights of victory. Everybody loves the rags to riches story. Many will tell of the hardships they encountered and roadblocks that seem higher than Mt. Everest on their journey to victory. One particular man brought tears to my eyes while writing this book, and his name is *Les Brown.*

Les is an excellent inspirational speaker. His life began at birth in an abandoned building in Miami, Florida. His mother had conceived him and his twin brother outside of wedlock while her husband was at war. Les and his brother were given up for adoption. Les was labeled in school as the *"dumb twin"* because his academics were far less than his brother's. Then one day, a teacher made a profound statement to him that changed the thought process of his life; and I want to share that with you because it holds true for all of us. He told Less, **"Someone's opinion of you does not have to become your reality!"**

You are your future; you create it and nobody else. Those are powerful words to live by, especially when *unplugging* from your past.

Today Les has written books, spoke for several Fortune Five Hundred companies, and has appeared on television numerous times. Les has an incredible testimony of how he *unplugged from his past* and built his future. If you dream it, you can achieve it, and with hard work, you can become it.

My passion is writing and wanting to help people with my books. I'm not smart; some might even call me dumb, for I pale compared to the intellectual. I never finished high school or attended a formal writing class. The patriarch Jacob, who found himself in an unpleasant situation in life, made this statement: *"All these things are against me."* There are times in life you can feel like everything is against you. The four walls are cascading on top of you, and there's more month than there is money. Yes, I lack scholastic ability, and my past does not hail from an Ivy League school or the affluent. My faith is in God, and what I believe He has called me to do, is greater than the past and my inabilities. Your past does not define you; it only propels you to become greater than what you were!

At times, I still have those voices of self-doubt and unbelief screaming in my head. Reminding me of who I am and where I lack. However, you have hope and consolation through the Word of God to combat this negativity. The Apostle John penned on his parchment, *"Greater is He that is in you, then he that is in the world" (1John 4:4)*. God in you is greater than all of the world's voices and the ones in your head. God tells you can succeed; its mind over matter. In this case, the "matter" is your past. Tell yourself you can, and you will.

It's the Apostle Paul, revered by many as one of the greatest Apostles in the New Testament, whose *"past"* could have held them back from their *"future"* in God. Paul would write fourteen of the twenty-seven books of the New Testament. His past was less than stellar, and it would be a thorn in his flesh that he would live with for the rest of his life, by his own admission. He sought the Lord for deliverance, and the Lord's response was simple, *"My Grace Is Sufficient for Thee, For My Strength Is Made Perfect In Weakness."* Your past is your weakness, but it can become your strength through Christ with His Word and His Spirit. Let's look at Paul's past.

PAUL'S PAST (SAUL)

And cast him out of the city, and stoned him: and the witnesses laid down their clothes at a young man's feet, whose name was Saul. And they stoned Stephen, Saul was consenting unto his death.

— *Acts 7:58-59, 8:1*

As for Saul, he made havoc of the church, entering into every house, and haling men and women committed them to prison.

— *Acts 8:3*

Saul, yet breathing out threatenings and slaughter against the disciples of the Lord.

— *Acts 9:1*

And I persecuted this way unto the death, binding and delivering into prisons both men and women.

— *Acts 22:4*

Many of the saints did I shut up in prison, having received authority from the chief priests; and when they were put to death, I gave my voice against them.

And I punished them oft in every synagogue, and compelled them to blaspheme; and being exceedingly mad against them, I persecuted them even unto strange cities.

— Acts 26:10-11

Wow! Talk about a past of regrets. No one would have ever suspected Paul to be a prime candidate for authoring two-thirds of the New Testament, and no one ever expected greatness out of your life either. But what they don't know is, God is prepping you for it.

Paul's past reminded him of who he used to be, but he couldn't allow the past mistakes to control and sabotage his future in God—neither can you. Paul's confession bore the sentiments of his heart. Acknowledging the *"past"* but refusing it to rule the *"future."* Don't let the scorning of your *"past"* predict your *"future."* Etch the words of the following scripture into your heart and recite them to yourself as many times as it takes until you believe them unequivocally.

"Brethren, I count not myself to have apprehended: but this one thing I do, forgetting those things which are behind, and reaching forth unto those things which are before,"
"I press toward the mark for the prize of the high calling of God in Christ Jesus."

— Philippians 3:13-14

There's a high calling on your life, and don't let the past ruin it. Paul had people put to death for their faith. The very people he once tried to destroy were now the ones he was preaching to, about a God that forgave him, saved him, and changed him.

The Gospel of Jesus Christ is the only thing that can take any seemingly hopeless situation and make it hopeful again. Like Paul, Manasseh, you, and I, there are things from the past that will try to haunt you and keep you trapped in the guilt of them.

Do I wish I could undo my wrongs and the mistakes I've made along the way? Of course, I do, but that's impossible. The only thing I can do is what Paul wrote about himself, and what you need to tell yourself when those thoughts try to bring you back, into the bondage of the past, "*forgetting those things which are behind, and reaching forth unto those things which are before*" *(Philippians 3:13)*.

Do I think Paul made mistakes after his conversion? I'm almost certain he did because humanity, by default, is programmed to fail. Failure is not the end; it's only a stepping-stone of growth. The Bible shows you that man failed in the very beginning. You will fail at times, but God is the remedy for your failures. God will never destroy somebody who fails because He knows they will get back up and rise again, through faith and belief in His Word.

> *For a just man falleth seven times, and riseth up again:*
> *— Prov 24:16*

THE FUTURE

> *There is therefore now no condemnation to them which are in Christ Jesus, who walk not after the flesh, but after the Spirit.*
> *— Romans 8:1*

The only escape from the past is to live for the future in Christ. God has not handed down a verdict damning you to be banished from His kingdom because of your past; He erased it in the waters of baptism. Stay in Christ, and continue to walk in faith through His Word, and you will be victorious.

> *(For the weapons of our warfare are not carnal, but mighty through God to the pulling down of strong holds;)*

*Casting down imaginations, and every high thing that
exalteth itself against the knowledge of God, and bringing
into captivity every thought to the obedience of Christ;*
*And having in a readiness to revenge all disobedience,
when your obedience is fulfilled.*

— 2 Corinthians 10:4-6

The *"past"* is a stronghold of your imagination that wants to enslave
you to your failures. This war cannot be fought with natural warfare, but
it is a spiritual battle in your mind. However, when you cast down those
self-deprecating thoughts that say your failure is greater than God's grace,
the tide will turn in your favor, and this is what Paul meant by having a
"readiness to revenge all disobedience."

Webster's Dictionary defines *"Readiness"* as the following:
- Prepared mentally or physically for some experience or action

You may feel mentally or physically inept, but God will be your
strength in this war. Like the premise of this book, you're sick and tired
of being sick and tired, and you're standing on the edge of the great divide
between "freedom and bondage." In the contemplative mind, you wrestle
with the fear of the unknown. Trusting God *(freedom)* and the battle of
wanting to cling to the security of your "past" *(bondage)*. However, no
longer will you vacillate between the two narratives of human reasoning
(your thoughts) and spiritual reasoning *(God's Word)*. Your mind is made
up, you're trusting God. The readiness you possess is the willingness of
a made-up mind to endure whatever you have to, to get what God has
promised you.

Strong's Concordance defines *"Revenge"* as the following:
- to vindicate, retaliate, punish:

Revenge is the war against the inner demons that want to rule your soul; it's the vindication of obedience. No longer will the resentments, bitterness, and jealousy of the past have dominion over you. Like the saying goes, *"it's time to clean the house,"* and that's what Manasseh did. He "cleaned the house," and it's time for you to do the same thing. Below is Manasseh's house cleaning; it's a detailed plan he implemented in his spiritual restoration.

> *Now after this he built a wall without the city of David, and raised it up a very great height, and put captains of war in all the fenced cities of Judah. He took away the strange gods, and the idol out of the house of the LORD, and all the altars that he had built in the mount of the house of the LORD, and in Jerusalem, and cast them out of the city And he repaired the altar of the LORD, and sacrificed thereon peace offerings and thank offerings, and commanded Judah to serve the LORD God of Israel. Nevertheless, the people did sacrifice still in the high places, yet unto the LORD their God only. Now the rest of the acts of Manasseh, and his prayer unto his God, and the words of the seers that spake to him in the name of the LORD God of Israel, behold, they are written in the book of the kings of Israel. His prayer also, and how God was intreated of him, and all his sin, and his trespass, and the places wherein he built high places, and set up groves and graven images, before he was humbled.*
> *– 2 Chronicles 33:14-19*

Your *future* begins with *unplugging from the past* and getting yourself right with God. When you line up your life with His Word, a made-up mind *(readiness)*, to destroy *(revenge)*, the things that tried to kill you, you are creating an atmosphere of victory for your life. Obeying the Word and cleaning our spiritual house (your mind) is the first step. When you humble yourself and get your heart right with the Lord, like Manasseh and many others you read about in the Bible, your future is filled with His blessing. You will still have some rough days; it's called life. But, there is no battle that you will lose or a war you can't win when God is fighting with you. So, let the celebrating begin of a new future by taking the first step by *"Unplugging from the past!"*

CHAPTER 6

YE SONS OF JACOB

Not in every case are you the predator, but in fact, for some, it was just the opposite; you were the prey. Maybe, you were made fun of in school because of your appearance or the clothes you wore? You suffered from being bullied, and maybe as a child, you were, or possibly still are, overweight, and those hurts have caused you to be insecure, and you've carried them your entire life. Maybe, you weren't popular in school and suffered because you were never invited to events and felt like an outcast? Perhaps, financially your family struggled, and you were embarrassed by them because of the house you lived in or the car they drove? Maybe, as a child you were sexually abused, and you've hidden it from everybody? Maybe, you've walked around with the pain and guilt bottled up inside of you and have felt ashamed of it? Possibly, your father or mother left you at a young age, and you haven't seen them since, and you've grown up wondering why? Do you feel like maybe you were the reason they left?

Whatever the case may be, it's painful to *unplug* from the anguish of it. It doesn't happen overnight. The intent of this book is to help you discover and address *"it."* I want to help you take the necessary steps to ensure victory by *unplugging from "it."*

Outside of the Lord, nobody like Joseph had to deal with the ill-treatment and pain caused by the ones Joseph loved the most—his family. One of the things that I made a very conscious effort as a parent was never to have favorites when having multiple children. Faith, our second daughter, was born thirteen months after our first daughter Sam. Sam was a very demanding child that commanded her mother's attention 24/7. So, I took care of Faith when I got home from work because Laura was exhausted from tending to two crying babies, thirteen months apart. Faith is what you would call a daddy's girl, and Sam is a mommy's girl. Boaz, our youngest, is a rainbow baby; but he's not favored above his siblings. However, seeing how he is the only boy, he's his Father's pride and his Mother's joy.

Sometimes things happen in a home that causes one child to be favored above the other, whether it's because of academics, athletics, appearance, etc., and they excel above their siblings. This should never occur under any circumstance. Sadly, it's not uncommon, and it even happened in biblical days; the *"favorite child"* syndrome.

I had the proclivity when I was younger that people in the Bible lived a perfect life. As I got older and began to read it, I soon discovered that wasn't the case at all. Delving into the scriptures and into the lives of whom the pages are filled with, you soon realize they are no different from you and me. Some of those people have absolutely insane childhoods that include: siblings murdering siblings, sexual assault among siblings, hatred towards siblings, daughter-in-laws having children fathered by their father-in-law's. These types of childhoods are not typical by any means and far from perfect. One such case comes from the household of Jacob and his sons.

> *Now Israel loved Joseph more than all his children, because he was the son of his old age: and he made him a coat of many colours. And when his brethren saw that their father*

loved him more than all his brethren, they hated him, and could not speak peaceably unto him.

— Genesis 37:3-4

Gen 37:3-4 shows you the hurts this causes in children when one feels less than the other. If anybody could relate to dealing with family issues and experiencing the hurts of the favorite child syndrome, Jacob would be. After all, Jacob's twin brother, Esau, was his father's favorite, *And Isaac loved Esau because he did eat of his venison (Genesis 25:28).* The scripture never says that Isaac loved Jacob (I'm sure he did). But it is quick to point this out because Esau had a special relationship with his father that Jacob didn't. Esau was the one that his father taught him to hunt. Like his father, Esau was a man of the field while Jacob stayed with his mother, tending to the home's things.

No child wants to feel less loved than his or her other siblings. I have seen this in families and the hurts it caused in the other children. The sons of Jacob were no exception. They noticed Joseph's special treatment, the affection Joseph got from their father that they wanted. The coat of many colors was the icing on the cake that ignited their hurts and fueled their anger.

Yes, Joseph was born to Jacob in his old age; for years, Jacob and Rachel had tried to have children and were unable, so when Joseph was born, he was special to them. Still, this didn't change the fact that Jacob's other sons wanted the same love and attention their father had given to Joseph.

Jacob and his sons were quite the motley crew. A family with some serious problems, and by any standard, they would be classified as a "dysfunctional home." They were, by no means, "normal."

It started with their father Jacob, and his mischievous and deceptive ways, swindling Esau out of his birthright and his father's inheritance. Simeon and Levi, Jacob's sons, kill a village of men because one of them raped their sister. Reuben Jacob's oldest son sexually assaults Jacob's concubine Bilhah (his brother's Dan, and Naphtali's mother). Two of Judah's sons are killed by God for their wickedness in his sight. Because of envy and jealousy, Jacob's ten sons plot to kill Joseph, but instead, sell him off as a slave to the Midianites and fabricating a lie to their father, saying Joseph was killed by a beast to cover up their sin. They had some serious issues going on in their household. Not exactly what you would expect for building materials to be used by God to become the greatest nation on the planet. They definitely had some family issues, and by no means would you classify their home life as *"normal."*

Yet, with all its insanity, this family would become the very nation God himself would descend from to redeem with His own blood. Don't sell yourself short because you didn't have the best upbringing or your past isn't spotless. God's own grandparents were *"dysfunctional."*

Like Jacob's household, there is *"dysfunction"* within many families today, and typically you see similar results. If you were to take a prison survey, I would venture to say most of its occupants come from a *"dysfunctional"* home. The world has become numb to *"dysfunction"* and accepts it as the *"norm."* The Wall Street Journal recently posted an article entitled; "marriage Is out of fashion." The mainstream media has downplayed the importance of family values and their structure as a moral society's building blocks; they continue to glorify the illicit lifestyles of high-society, plastering their debauchery all over the tabloids. They sensationalize ungodliness, and they look down on morality.

When a child grows up in a dysfunctional house, the cards by default are stacked against them. Often, *"dysfunction"* is perceived as the *"norm,"* and the cycle will continue. For example, the little boy who grows up seeing his father abuse his mother, verbally or physically, perceives this as how women are treated and do the same thing with his wife. A little girl growing up watching her mother show no respect to her father, and berating him later in life, will do the same to her husband. The cycle continues, and it's only God who can stop this viciousness and truly break the chains of *"dysfunction."*

On the next block over from my house, where I grew up, was a foster home. One young girl who had recently been placed there while I was in my ninth-grade year comes to mind. She was a nice girl, and she became popular with the boys rather quickly. At the time, I didn't realize how foster care worked, nor did I really stop to think about it. This young girl's painful reality had come from a broken home; something terrible had happened in her life that forced her to live in a Foster Home. In hindsight, I can see that her actions spoke volumes for the longing for love from the male figure missing in her life. Her popularity with the boys resulted in teenage pregnancy. She and the father married, but it didn't last. They ended up getting a divorce, and the cycle continued.

I am the result of adolescent pregnancy. Like so many others, I know what it's like to live in *dysfunction*. My dad was a senior in high school at the time of my birth. My mom, on the other hand, was forced to drop out of school to take care of her dying mother, along with being pregnant. My parents got married, moved into an apartment, and worked nights at the local grocery store, and went to school during the day.

They had tried, but at such a young age, it just didn't work out. They got divorced, and my father was granted custody of me. Often, I would stay with my grandparents because my dad wanted to go out and enjoy his life. After all, he was only 22 years old with a three-year-old son. They say memories are directly attached to emotions. Believe it or not, at the age of three, I can still remember the night my mom left my dad and me.

My parents had been fighting that night, and my mom decided she would leave. Somehow at the age of 3, I knew she wasn't coming back. She stormed out of the dining room, headed towards the front door, opened it, walked out, and slammed it shut. I remember running towards her as the door shut and standing against it, with my hands and face pressed against its cold surface. Tears streamed down my face and the doors. Until

I was probably 6 or 7, I don't remember my mother being a part of my life. Something happened inside me that day, and at the time, I didn't know what it was, but now I do; it's called anger. It's a stronghold that had placed a base in my heart that would alter my life forever.

Around the age of 10, my father remarried. Through that marriage, I got a wonderful stepsister Erika, who would become as close to me as any biological sister could ever be, and a new half-sister Ivonne, who was the cutest kid ever. At first, this was a beautiful thing, a new beginning, a new home, a fresh start. We moved away from our small hometown to Harper Woods, MI (a suburb outside of Detroit). I met new friends, went to a new school, seen another side of the world that I had never witnessed before. The houses were stacked side by side, unlike the rural town I grew up in, the yards were small with minimal upkeep, and we played baseball in the street. This suburban lifestyle expanded my scope of life as a ten-year-old boy from the rural town of Imlay City, MI. I had never seen a two-story elementary school or a class of three hundred plus students in it. The world had just been opened up to me. My small box of youthful perception had just been blown up to epic proportions. It was surreal to me, the hustle and bustle of the city life; I loved it.

As time would tell, a horrible manifestation would appear in my father's new marriage --my stepmother was an alcoholic. Her adaptation to the respectability of marriage and having a family was a struggle. It became a losing battle that she would surrender to an addiction that would cost her both of her daughters one day. One night, she was drunk and driving us kids (to of all places, Wednesday night bible study). All of a sudden, she slammed on the brakes to prevent herself from rear-ending a car. As the car came to a screeching halt, a whiskey bottle rolled out from under my seat. I looked down at the bottle that had just come to rest between my feet and just stared at it in wonderment. My sisters didn't see it, and my stepmother was so drunk I knew she didn't realize that her reckless driving had catapulted the bottle from under the seat where she had hidden it. At that very moment, something in my heart grabbed ahold of me (like anger did) and said, "You've to try this." Even though I knew this very substance was destroying our home, I thought maybe this could be a temporary escape. I waited until that night after everybody went to bed, then I crept downstairs to retrieve the mysterious bottle. I wanted to drink it. I wanted to *"unplug"* from the drama that had become my world. To my dismay, the bottle was gone. As her addiction began to appear more and more, so did the fighting.

Their marriage would begin to descend at an alarming rate. By the time it hit the ground, there was carnage everywhere. Like Humpty Dumpty, the pieces couldn't be put back together again. The day finally came when the fighting reached its breaking point. The wedding rings were thrown on the kitchen table. It was over. As I watched my stepmother get into her car, a cold-blooded hatred for her seared through my veins. I stared at my sister through my upstairs bedroom as they were driving off with my stepmother to God only knows where. I knew this was the end.

I found myself alone, angry, and hurting. The inevitable was coming. I looked around my room at my posters on the walls and the bed I knew I would never sleep in again. The anger I felt when I was a child had now cemented itself even deeper in my heart. I had grown to hate my stepmom. Her Janus-faced ways had made me very bitter towards her (and women in general). She was Dr. Jekyll and Mr. Hyde. She was a brilliant actor. She was kind and would be overly sweet around my father, never revealing the lurking rage she had towards me in front of him. Her favorite form of discipline was writing lines. On one particular incident, in a fit of rage and drunkenness, she got within an inch of my face and said, *"I hate you,"* and in my heart, I yelled back, *"I HATE YOU!"* I was probably around the age of thirteen when this happened, and later that night, when my dad got home, it was like nothing had ever happened.

Dad called me to the kitchen where the fighting had just ended and told me to call my friends and say my goodbyes. We were leaving and never returning. Mike Watson, my best friend at the time, came over to the house, and we were standing outside of the laundry room. Mike asked me what was going on; I rehashed the series of events that had just transpired. Our friendship had come to an end. It was a sad moment for Mike and me. I would miss him dearly *(this was before the days of texting and social media)*. I wouldn't see Mike until years later when I could drive. We said our goodbyes, and Mike got on his bike, and I watched him ride down the driveway for the last time in my life.

I returned to my bedroom, finished packing my clothes, loaded up the suburban, and we left that day. I never again stepped foot in that house I once called home. As we pulled out of the driveway and headed down the street, I can remember peering out the window as we drove by the houses I had walked past every day for years on my way to and from school, thinking to myself, "I'll never see these again."

I have driven through our old neighborhood as a grown man when working in the area on many occasions. Every time I drive through our old neighborhood, and the places I used to play as a boy growing up, all the memories come flooding back to me like the day they happened. Our house doesn't look the same as it did when we lived there. They put new siding on it, tore down the garage, and put a privacy fence around the yard. I can remember the countless football and wiffleball games we played at our house and the time my dad busted one of my friends smoking behind the garage.

All the things I did in our neighborhood that were once a part of my life are now only memories. They are reborn at the passing of my father, coupled with writing the account of them—never during those times could I've imagined one day I'd be writing about them in this book.

This is not an uncommon story today, and it seems to be more normal than the abnormal. I know many people that share the same story, teenage pregnancy, parents got divorced, later got remarried, and then got divorced again. Even from the beginning, families had drama, and "dysfunction" existed in the home. For example, the first family ever created Adam and Eve and their sons, Cain and Abel. Cain murders Abel because of jealously, and rejection and the cycle began.

"When Joseph's brethren saw that their father loved him more than all his brethren, they hated him, and could not speak peaceably unto him" (Genesis 37:4). Joseph, Jacob's youngest son, lost his mother early and was raised by his stepmother, Leah. Joseph felt jealousy from his half-brothers because his father favored him, but this wasn't his fault. This was a grave mistake on Jacob's part, but Jacob was hurting because he loved Rachel, and Joseph was the first child they had together. When Jacob gave Joseph the coat of many colors, it was the tipping point of his brothers' bitterness.

Being a stepchild, you can see and feel the difference in love. The actions that come from a stepparent and the affection towards their biological children are different. I can attest to this, and so can my sisters. And that's not to say that the stepparent doesn't love you, but there is a deeper bond when it's biological. This is pure speculation, but Leah may have favored her sons above Joseph, and he felt the separation. After all, Joseph wasn't her son, and Leah could see the favoritism Jacob had for him above her sons. *Unplugging* from such hurts can take time, weeks, months, even years when the wounds are so deep.

Watching my son being raised with his mother in his life, receiving her love and nurturing, has had an enormous impact on shaping and forming him into the young man he has become. I can now see the importance of how impactful a mother's love is in her son's life. Not being raised by my mother and an abusive stepmother (my father's second wife), with no love and nurturing from either one, would be the foundation for bitterness in me towards women. It would take me years to *unplug* from a lack of respect for women and learning to appreciate them and their roles.

A VISION FOR THE FUTURE

Gods got a calling and a purpose for your life like he did Joseph's. Like Joseph, the things you've gone through are steppingstones, not stumbling blocks, for your future. In the end, Joseph understood that God used all this to make him a better person. Paul said, *"All Things Work Together for Good" (Romans 8:28)*. Everything in life that happens to you will either make or break you, whether good or bad. Your life and its end result are 90% of your personal choices and 10% circumstances.

There are times in life where your vision becomes blurred by the storms. The endless waves of woe's that seem to billow over your head on the seas of life. These are the trying times of faith and trust in God. It's in these moments when your human reasoning can't understand why and how a loving God can allow such things to happen to you. *"Faith is rugged, and trust is forged in the furnace of fiery trials."*

Jesus never promised that the cross would not
get heavy or the hill hard to climb.
He never offered victory without fighting, but
He said help will always come in time.

God is an 11:59 pm God (if you don't know what that means, 11:59 pm is the moment just before the coup de grace is about to strike, God steps in and thwarts the impending doom). God has to allow certain things to happen in your life, as seen in the life of Joseph. To help you better understand that things are not always what they appear. The Apostle Luke wrote in the book of Acts and quoting from the Old Testament Prophet Joel, a promise that God gave to His Church.

"Your young men shall see visions, and your old men shall dream dreams."

— Acts 2:17

There have been many times in my life and in the lives of others who can testify that God has shown them things that they didn't understand at the time they were given. God gave me dreams years ago that I still don't know their interpretation to this day. Sometimes, it was not until years down the road that the dream or vision's intent and purpose were revealed. Thus, was the case with Joseph and the dreams God gave him for the future.

> *And Joseph dreamed a dream, and he told it his breth-ren: and they hated him yet the more. And he said unto them, Hear, I pray you, this dream which I have dreamed: For, behold, we were binding sheaves in the field, and, lo, my sheaf arose, and also stood upright; and, behold, your sheaves stood round about, and made obeisance to my sheaf. And his brethren said to him, Shalt thou indeed reign over us? or shalt thou indeed have dominion over us? And they hated him yet the more for his dreams, and for his words.*
> *– Genesis 37:5-8*

Not only did Joseph's brothers hate him because Joseph was his father's favorite son, but also because God was giving him dreams, and not them. Joseph recites his dreams to his brothers, and they would become enraged. Not only is Joseph loved above them, but it seemed that Joseph would one day have dominion over them too. Joseph didn't ask for the dreams; God gave them to him. People's animosity towards you because of something God gives you, and not them, will one day be their deliverance. Joseph's words only etched their hatred, deeper on the walls of resentment, in their heart against him.

Solomon writes in the Song of Solomon 8:6, *"jealousy is cruel as the grave"!* The cruelty of jealousy has led many lives into destruction, and the jealousy in the sons of Jacob was no different. Joseph's brother's hatred, coupled with jealousy towards their brother, propelled them to commit great evil against Joseph that he could never have imagined.

> *This I recall to my mind, therefore have I hope. It is of the LORD's mercies that we are not consumed because his compassions fail not. They are new every morning: great is thy faithfulness.*
>
> *— Laminations 3:21-23*

Little did Joseph or his brothers know that those dreams would be their future. If God used dreams with Joseph and many others in the Bible, He could use them with you for the benefit of helping His people. Great is the Lord's faithfulness towards His people. *"I am the LORD, I change not; therefore ye sons of Jacob are not consumed"* (Malachi 3:6). God will use whatever means He has to save a soul, even at the expense of using the jealousy of a brother against a brother or a sister against a sister, ye sons of Jacob have hope.

THE BETRAYAL OF A BROTHER

One can only speculate those dreams must have encouraged Joseph that better things were in store for him and his future. However, Joseph's brothers did not hide their feelings towards him or how they felt about his dreams. Joseph didn't realize that it would take him down a road of betrayal from his brothers for those dreams to come to pass. This is probably one of the hardest things in a relationship to *"unplug"* from. Betrayal is turning your back on someone. It's hurting the one who loves you and trusts you. Even though there was a conflict between Joseph and his brothers, he could never think to do them any harm. Unfortunately, the feelings weren't mutual.

For Joseph's dreams to become a reality, the wheels of motion had to turn in an adverse direction in his life. As fate would have it, one day, while Joseph was tending to the things of his life, Jacob summoned him to go look at the welfare of his brothers. Knowing they would be in the common grazing area of Shechem, Joseph made his way to their location. This day would be a day to remember, a day that would forever change Joseph and his family's life.

To Joseph, this started out as just any ordinary day, a hot, humid day and the occasional sudden dust storms that would arise in the prairies of Canaan. With his Shepherd's bag at his side and staff in hand, Joseph started out on his journey to Shechem. Upon arriving at Shechem, much to his surprise, his brothers were nowhere to be found. Puzzled by this, Joseph set out to start looking for them.

> *And a certain man found him, and, behold, he was wandering in the field: and the man asked him, saying, What seekest thou? And he said, I seek my brethren: tell me, I pray thee, where they feed their flocks. And the man said, They are departed hence; for I heard them say, Let us go to Dothan. And Joseph went after his brethren and found them in Dothan.*
>
> *– Genesis 37:15-17*

In the next reading section, you'll see where letting anger, jealousy, and bitterness takes a person who refuses to let go and let God. Harboring ill feelings will only make your life more miserable and cause you to do things you'll regret later in life, but this had to happen. God had to use their wickedness to bring their deliverance.

> *And when they saw him afar off, even before he came near unto them, they conspired against him to slay him. And they said one to another, "Behold, this dreamer cometh." "Come now, therefore, and let us slay him, and cast him into*

some pit, and we will say, some evil beast hath devoured him:
and we shall see what will become of his dreams."

Reuben heard it, and he delivered him out of their
hands; and said, "Let us not kill him." And Reuben said
unto them, "Shed no blood, but cast him into this pit that is
in the wilderness, and lay no hand upon him;" that he might
rid him out of their hands, to deliver him to his father again.

I don't believe Reuben had a pure motive to deliver Joseph out of their hands because he loved him. I think Reuben's reasons were selfish; he would use this as a ploy to gain his father's forgiveness, for the betrayal that he committed against him, for his wife's sexual assault. He possibly feared somehow, Jacob would find out he had his hand in Joseph's death, and he would forever be hated by his father.

And it came to pass when Joseph was come unto his
brethren, that they stript Joseph out of his coat, his coat of
many colors that was on him. They took him, and cast him
into a pit: and the pit was empty, there was no water in it.

Then they sat down to eat bread: and they lifted up their
eyes and looked, and, behold, a company of Ishmeelites came
from Gilead with their camels bearing spicery and balm and
myrrh, going to carry it down to Egypt.

Judah said unto his brethren, "What profit is it if we
slay our brother, and conceal his blood?" "Come, and let
us sell him to the Ishmeelites, and let not our hand be upon
him; for he is our brother and our flesh." And his brethren
were content.

Then there passed by Midianites merchantmen, and they
drew and lifted up Joseph out of the pit, and sold Joseph to

the Ishmeelites for twenty pieces of silver: and they brought Joseph into Egypt".

— Genesis 37:15-28

Their cruel act of hatred, and betrayal, towards Joseph, would leave a scar for life. Selling him for a slave would be the beginning of a trial that Joseph would endure for over twenty years. You can imagine Joseph's deafening cries, as he pleads for his brother's help, fell on deaf ears as he watched their silhouettes fade in the distance. Joseph was headed to a destination he had never been to before; he'd only heard of the mystical place called Egypt.

Try to imagine the mind of a seventeen-year-old boy as he approached the land of Egypt. The golden city of radiant splendor and the effulgence's were beyond anything Joseph had ever seen. As they drew near the mysterious place, he could see the towering statues of their pagan deities in the distance. It displayed brilliant craftsmanship and skill that transformed a piece of stone into a detailed god. Passing by the Nile River, beholding all the ships laden with cargo, importing, and exporting their goods, was something Joseph had never witnessed before growing up in the desert. It was the metropolis of the world. He had only heard tales of the mysterious place, but now it was no longer a mystery. It was now a reality. Just hours before, he was with his family and caring for his father's sheepfold. Joseph thought about his father and how he would be worried about him because he had been gone for so long. How would his brothers explain his disappearance? What fallacy would they fabricate to cover up the truth? As the harsh reality crashed down on top of him, Joseph now found himself standing on an auction block perplexed by these thoughts.

Potiphar, an officer of Pharaoh, captain of the guard, an Egyptian, bought him of the hands of the Ishmeelites, which had brought him down thither. The LORD was with Joseph, and he was a prosperous man; and he was in the house of his master the Egyptian. And his master saw that the LORD was with him, and that the LORD made all that he did to prosper in his hand. And Joseph found grace in his sight, and he served him: and he made him overseer over his house, and all that he had he put into his hand. And it came to pass from the time that he had made him overseer in his house, and over all that he had, that the LORD blessed the Egyptian's house for Joseph's sake; and the blessing of the LORD was upon all that he had in the house, and in the field. And he left all that he had in Joseph's hand; and he knew not ought he had, save the bread which he did eat. And Joseph was a goodly person, and well favoured.

– Genesis 39:1-6

Life for Joseph wasn't that bad; he was a domestic slave, unlike those around him who were purchased to work tilling the ground or in the mud pits. For the first time since his brothers' betrayal when they sold him as a slave to the Ishmeelites, things started to go right for Joseph. No matter what he did, it always worked out. Joseph soon began to realize that God was with him. Life in Egypt was taking on a new outlook. Joseph was elevated to "overseer" of his master's house, and it also brought privileges beyond the standard living of a slave. I believe Joseph had been granted the freedom to explore and understand the Egyptian culture because his master trusted him. Joseph began to learn the Egyptian language, fished the Nile River, and experienced an eatery he'd never tasted before. Egypt was a wonder like nothing he'd ever seen before. This was a far cry from being a sheepherder.

There is that old saying we've heard many times in life, *"it's too good to be true."* As fate would have it, *"things were too good to be true."* Joseph had sensed something odd about how his master's wife had been smiling at him whenever she talked to him. She began to ask him to do things out of the ordinary, which made him uncomfortable.

Then his worst fear came to pass;

> *his master's wife cast her eyes upon Joseph; and she said, "Lie with me."*
>
> *But he refused, and said unto his master's wife, "Behold, my master wotteth not what is with me in the house, and he hath committed all that he hath to my hand;*
>
> *There is none greater in this house than I; neither hath he kept back anything from me but thee, because thou art his wife: how then can I do this great wickedness and sin against God"?*
>
> *– Genesis39:7-9*

In disbelief, Joseph couldn't believe his ears. To commit such a sin against Potiphar was unthinkable --she was relentless in her pursuit! *And it came to pass, as she spake to Joseph day by day that he hearkened not unto her, to lie by her, or to be with her (Genesis 39:10).* Joseph's joy and freedom, along with the trust of his master, were now in jeopardy. Life became drudgery as he walked on pins and needles because his master's wife taunted and flirted with Joseph every day, trying to entice him. Yet Joseph thwarted her attempts and maintained his integrity with Potiphar. Then his worst fear became his reality; *One day, Joseph went into the house to do his business, and there was none of the men of the house there within. And she caught him by his garment, saying, "Lie with me:" and he left his garment in her hand, and fled, and got him out. (Genesis 39:10-11).*

Alone outside of the house, trembling, his mind was gripped with fear. Could this be the end of his life? Would he ever get out of this place alive? Would he ever see his father again? Why was this happening to him? No matter what was said, Potiphar wouldn't believe him. He was a dead man! As the minutes seemed to turn to hours, the trepidation of Potiphar's return was agonizing. Potiphar was the chief of the executioners, and surely, he would have Joseph put to death.

When reading the account of Joseph's life, it will take you back. Joseph's life is marked with extremities. For the first half of his life, Joseph is plagued with hatred and jealousy from the ones he loves the most. Now his life is flashing before his eyes, and yet again, betrayal has not only destroyed his life before but, this time, it may cost him his life. The bible doesn't give you the conversation between Potiphar and Joseph. Judging by what happened, intuitively, Potiphar knew Joseph was innocent, but for the sake of his wife's honor, Potiphar had to punish Joseph. So, rather than putting him to death, he imprisoned him. *Joseph's master took him, and put him into the prison, a place where the king's prisoners were bound: and he was there in the prison (Genesis 39:20).*

Joseph's life had been spared. However, he had been lied about, falsely accused, and imprisoned for a crime he never committed. All of this brought back to the surface his anger towards his brothers for their injurious deeds. Once again, Joseph is faced with the painful sting of betrayal, like the day he watched his brothers exchange money for his soul. Betrayal is one of the hardest things to *"unplug"* from.

Unplugging from betrayal means that you have to let down the security walls you have built up that prevent anybody from entering into your heart, including God. They've become fortified and impenetrable. You know God sees and knows all things before they ever happen, and your humanity questions why He allows such things to happen, knowing they bring such pain? You question His Love...You question His Word...You question His existence in your life at these moments, and so did Joseph.

THINGS ARE NOT ALWAYS WHAT THEY APPEAR, IT'S CALLED "A SET-UP"

As Joseph is sitting in his cell feeling hopeless and unsure, the thought of rotting away in prison for a crime he didn't commit became overwhelming. Joseph asked himself this question, "why, why God, why me?" Like Joseph, you may often ask yourself this question as you sit in your cell of hopelessness. The feelings of uncertainty and "why, why God, why me?" race through your head. Feeling like this is unfair, cruel, and not the love of God, you begin to lose your trust in Him.

I've had my *"why God"* moments in life. Shortly after the 9/11 attacks, I went from having 12 employees to just me and a brother from church, Ed Brown. My life felt like it was turned upside down and being crushed by the I.R.S... Everything I worked so hard to build with my company was gone. I found myself reeling in a sea of despair. The interest and penalties from the I.R.S. were mounting, and as one debt was getting paid off, the others kept growing at an alarming rate. It seemed like God was nowhere to be found; I felt deserted by Him. I questioned if the bible was even real. Everything I knew was now being tested as I battled, feeling like God had betrayed me. One day, Ed and I were installing a roof on a home, and I was expressing my internal struggles and my faith in God; he stopped in the middle of what he was doing and looked at me and said, *"Tommy, you've got to trust God, even when it seems like He's not there; He's there."* Within myself, I said, *"I just don't know?"*

I'll never forget that low point in my life. Out of destruction can come construction because things are not always what they appear, my friend. This book is a part of the reconstruction process that started on that roof. Out of destruction, God will start construction; nothing is for naught in God. With God, you never lose if you never quit.

However, unbeknownst to Joseph would be the beginning of a greater calling God was preparing him for in his prison cell.

Things may have happened in your life that you don't understand, but things are not always what they seem. God is preparing you for your calling. God sent Joseph to prison to prepare him for what was about to happen in his life. God is preparing each and every one of us to be used in our calling. Your experiences and the trials/tribulations, like Joseph, will be the salvation of others. It wasn't long before the ebbs and flows began to change for the better in the tide of Joseph's life. Just like the strange occurrences that happened in Potiphar's house, they began to happen again in prison. Joseph began to realize that the Lord's hand was with him.

The LORD was with Joseph, and shewed him mercy, and gave him favour in the sight of the keeper of the prison (Genesis 39:21). The favor was a ray of light in a dim situation. Your spark of light will spring from the shadows of nowhere because God loves His people, and God gave a promise to you --He would never leave you or forsake you. Even in prison, God was with Joseph, and in your prison, God is with you.

> *"Let us not be weary in well doing: for **in due season ye shall reap** if ye faint not."*
> *– Galatians 6:9*

The Bible doesn't tell you how long Joseph was in prison before anything beyond his wildest dreams would unravel. You may think your prison cell is the end, but really, it is the *"setup"* for something greater in your life. The storyline of Joseph's *"set up"* really began years before his imprisonment. It started when God gave him those dreams as a teenager. Joseph's dreams wouldn't come to pass until years later, and in those dreams, you see the end of the *"setup"* that God started in Joseph's life as a teenager. Just like Joseph, there are some things that God started in you a long time ago, and they haven't come to pass yet, but they will --a change of season is coming; just hold on.

And it came to pass after these things, that the butler of the king of Egypt and his baker had offended their lord the king of Egypt. And Pharaoh was wroth against two of his officers, against the chief of the butlers, and against the chief of the bakers. And he put them in ward in the house of the captain of the guard, into the prison, the place where Joseph was bound. And the captain of the guard charged Joseph with them, and he served them: and they continued a season in ward. And they dreamed a dream both of them, each man his dream in one night, each man according to the interpretation of his dream, the butler and the baker of the king of Egypt, which were bound in the prison.

— Genesis 40:1-5

This day started out like any other day. Joseph had gotten word that they had some new arrivals in the jail, Pharoah's butler, and baker. By now, Joseph had climbed the ranks and was now a trustee. His job was tending to the welfare of the prisoners and their daily needs. Today, however, the new inmates seem disheveled, withdrawn, and to themselves. Joseph inquires.

And Joseph came in unto them in the morning, and looked upon them, and, behold, they were sad. And he asked Pharaoh's officers that were with him in the ward of his lord's house, saying," Wherefore look ye so sadly to day?"

And they said unto him, "We have dreamed a dream, and there is no interpreter of it." And Joseph said unto them, "do not interpretations belong to God? Tell me them, I pray you."

And the chief butler told his dream to Joseph, and said to him, "In my dream, behold, a vine was before me; And in the vine were three branches: and it was as though it budded, and her blossoms shot forth; and the clusters thereof brought forth ripe grapes: And Pharaoh's cup was in my hand: and I took the grapes, and pressed them into Pharaoh's cup, and I gave the cup into Pharaoh's hand."

And Joseph said unto him, "This is the interpretation of it: The three branches are three days:" "Yet within three days shall Pharaoh lift up thine head, and restore thee unto thy place: and thou shalt deliver Pharaoh's cup into his hand, after the former manner when thou wast his butler." "But think on me when it shall be well with thee, and shew kindness, I pray thee, unto me, and make mention of me unto Pharaoh, and bring me out of this house:" "For indeed I was stolen away out of the land of the Hebrews: and here also have I done nothing that they should put me into the dungeon."

When the chief baker saw that the interpretation was good, he said unto Joseph, "I also was in my dream, and, behold, I had three white baskets on my head:"

'And in the uppermost basket there was of all manner of bakemeats for Pharaoh; and the birds did eat them out of the basket upon my head."

And Joseph answered and said, "This is the interpretation thereof: The three baskets are three days." "Yet within three days shall Pharaoh lift up thy head from off thee, and shall hang thee on a tree; and the birds shall eat thy flesh from off thee."

And it came to pass the third day, which was Pharaoh's birthday, that he made a feast unto all his servants: and he lifted up the head of the chief butler and of the chief baker

among his servants. And he restored the chief butler unto his
butlership again; and he gave the cup into Pharaoh's hand:
But he hanged the chief baker: as Joseph had interpreted
to them. Yet did not the chief butler remember Joseph, but
forgat him.

— Genesis 40:6-23

Allow me once again to step out on a limb here, but, I have to believe as the words flowed out of Joseph's mouth with the interpretation of the dreams, the Spirit of the Almighty God touched his soul. Never in Joseph's life had he ever interpreted a dream. Somehow, Joseph knew this would be the beginning of something far greater down the road.

Looking back, God has shown you things that you didn't understand at the time, and maybe you still don't now. Don't worry, be patient, and wait on the Lord because He will show you in time what it means. It's just not the perfect timing, that's all.

Call it evangelistic or reading between the lines, but I believe word got around the prison about what happened to the butler and the baker. Joseph's interpretations of their dreams had come to pass. Amazed beyond words and awestruck, God had given Joseph the explanations of their dreams. As word traveled of their fate, simultaneously, sadness and joy rushed through Joseph. He grieved the loss of the baker he predicted would die yet rejoiced at the news of the butler being restored. Joseph's heart leaped with joy, and again a ray of light sprang into the prison cell of his heart; inevitably, he was going to be released. At any moment, at any time, any day now, Joseph would be exonerated from a crime he didn't commit.

At last, freedom was within Joseph's grasp. Finally, he would be set free and return to his native land to be with his father. After all, it was Joseph who interpreted the butler's dream. Surely the butler would tell Pharaoh of Joseph's innocence. The butler knew Joseph was falsely

THOMAS L. TEAL JR

accused of a crime he didn't commit. Joseph had shared his life story with the butler, how he was sold-out by his brother to the slave traders. So, there Joseph sat, waiting patiently for his name to be called (figuratively). At any moment, he would be summoned to receive his release papers. Excitement overwhelmed him. Joseph was finally going home. So, he waited, and waited, and waited as the hours turned to days, and the days turned to weeks, and the weeks turned into months. Joseph's joy was fleeing, and the harsh reality was seeping into his soul. Joseph wasn't getting released, and worse yet, he wasn't going home.

These are some of the hardest times in life. God uses you to help someone else get their freedom and joy. You watch them get restored, and yet, you're still in a prison-cell of hopelessness. Wondering why? Why would God use you to help someone out of prison, and He leaves you in yours? The Paradox of *Unplugging*.

YOU HAVE TO "UNPLUG" FROM HURTS CAUSED BY OTHERS, BY LETTING GO, AND TRUSTING GOD!

Joseph was wasting away mentally and physically in that prison cell. Can you relate? Taunted by his thoughts, he wondered if he would ever be set free. Have you been there? Time was melting away, and so was Joseph; he had so many questions. Why did his brothers hate him so much? Why would the God of his fathers, the God of Abraham, Isaac, and Jacob, allow this to happen? How could his brothers be so cruel to him? What, because Joseph was their father's favorite son, that gave them permission to unleash their battery of cruelties towards him? Joseph was again fighting all the emotions from the past, as the possibility of being freed was dwindling away.

Likewise, you are wasting away mentally and physically in your prison cell of bitterness because of the wrongs people have done to you. Shackled in unforgiveness towards a spouse, sibling, or even a close friend who has hurt you, you are incarcerated with hatred. You hold on to your resentment feeling justified because of your violation. The longer you live in this state, the longer it will take to see freedom.

In prison, Joseph had a lot of time to think, and so do you. Like Joseph, you've been locked up for a crime you didn't commit. Now you're fighting for your freedom. More importantly, you're struggling to overcome the anger in your heart towards your offenders, those who have *betrayed* you.

You have one of two choices to make –

1. Hold on to the anger and hurts caused by others.
2. Forgive the hurts and pains caused by those people, and pray for them, and trust that God has allowed it to happen for a good reason!

2 Corinthians 5:18 says, *"All things are of God."* Good or bad, It's all of God, and you have to accept that, even when you find yourself in prison. Let go and trust God.

No better example epitomizes forgiving others who have *betrayed* them than the Lord Jesus Christ. Jesus Christ never assaulted anybody. He never lied to anybody. He never deceived anybody. No sin could be laid to His charge. Yet, they condemned Him to death for a crime He never committed. He was beaten beyond recognition, a crown of thorns was smashed on his head, Innumerable lacerations, and he hung on a cross to die. The Lord then makes the most astonishing statement ever made," *Father, forgive them, for they know not what they do" (Luke 23:34).*

Forgiving and letting go of hurts, and trusting God is not an easy process. It can take days, months, and even years, depending on the depth of pain. For Joseph, it would be twenty-plus years before he would face his brothers, and he would be tested to see if he really let go and trusted God.

"Take heed to yourselves: If thy brother trespass against thee, rebuke him; and if he repent, forgive him." "And if he

*trespass against thee seven times in a day, and seven times in
a day turn again to thee, saying, I repent; thou shalt forgive
him." And the apostles said unto the Lord, "Increase our
faith."*

– Luke 17:3-5

When someone has hurt you so severely, on multiple occasions, it
takes faith to believe that when they say, *"I'm sorry,"* that they are really
sorry. You want to forgive, and you want to believe they're sorry for what
they did, but it's hard. This is why the Apostles said, *"Lord Increase Our
Faith."* I want you to pray and ask the Lord the same thing, *"Lord, increase
my faith."* It takes faith beyond the pain to forgive and *unplug* because
forgetting betrayal is one of the hardest things to do. You have to let go
and trust God; it is the journey of *"unplugging"* and a part of the healing
process.

*It is of the LORD'S mercies that we are not consumed
because his compassions fail not.*

– Lamentations 3:22

*"I am the LORD, I change not; therefore ye sons of Jacob
are not consumed."*

– Malachi 3:6

CHAPTER 7

A CHANGE OF SEASON

"Weeping may endure for a night but joy cometh in the morning."

– Psalms 30:5

There are times in life where you have a ray of hope or even some type of financial opportunity arise to help in your difficult situation, only to have it vanish as fast as it appeared. The wind is knocked out of you, and you feel like you're being kicked while you're down. Things are not always going to stay this way. The sun will shine again. The Lord's capabilities are endless, and His means of deliverance are mind-boggling. In one moment, you can have a complete *change of season*. In one day, your life can be completely turned around.

You say to yourself, *"how do you know Tom?"* *"Weeping may endure for a night but joy cometh in the morning."* The morning is coming; it's just nighttime right now. God's Word does not lie. I've served the Lord for over half of my life, and I have seen the morning come, and so will you. It's in your trials and afflictions; he is setting up your *change of season.* James 1:3 says, *"Knowing this, that the trying of your faith worketh patience."* Trials are the building blocks of your spiritual foundation. Faith in God's promises is what He's looking for in what may appear to be a dim situation. Unbeknownst to you, behind the scenes, God is setting things up for your deliverance, like he did for Joseph.

Don't be weary in well-doing because it's time for a *change of season*. I'm sure there were times in Joseph's life where he wanted to give up because he grew tired during those lonely hours of waiting as time was melting away. It's in those lonely hours of your contemplation that God is grooming you for your *change of season* like He did for Joseph. Whether you realize it or not, God is with you. He is an omnipresent God. That means He's in all places at all times, including your "jail-cell."

> *And it came to pass at the end of two full years, that Pharaoh dreamed: and, behold, he stood by the river. And, behold, there came up out of the river seven well favoured kine and fatfleshed; and they fed in a meadow. And, behold, seven other kine came up after them out of the river, ill favoured and leanfleshed; and stood by the other kine upon the brink of the river. And the ill favoured and leanfleshed kine did eat up the seven well favoured and fat kine. So Pharaoh awoke.*
>
> *And he slept and dreamed the second time: and, behold, seven ears of corn came up upon one stalk, rank and good. And, behold, seven thin ears and blasted with the east wind sprung up after them. And the seven thin ears devoured the seven rank and full ears. And Pharaoh awoke, and, behold, it was a dream. And it came to pass in the morning that his spirit was troubled; and he sent and called for all the magicians of Egypt, and all the wise men thereof: and Pharaoh told them his dream; but there was none that could interpret them unto Pharaoh.*

Then spake the chief butler unto Pharaoh, saying, "I do remember my faults this day. Pharaoh was wroth with his servants, and put me in ward in the captain of the guard's house, both me and the chief baker: And we dreamed a dream in one night, I and he; we dreamed each man according to the interpretation of his dream. And there was there with us a young man, an Hebrew, servant to the captain of the guard; and we told him, and he interpreted to us our dreams; to each man according to his dream he did interpret. And it came to pass, as he interpreted to us, so it was; me he restored unto mine office, and him he hanged".

Then Pharaoh sent and called Joseph,

— Genesis 41:1-14

The distant sound of hurried footsteps, and the rumbling of multiple voices, were growing louder as their sound echoed off the prison walls. Suddenly, the doors were kicked wide open like a swat team executing a raid. Pharaoh's guards start screaming and yelling, *"WHERE IS THE HEBREW SLAVE? WHERE IS THE HEBREW SLAVE JOSEPH?"*

One can only imagine the fear and trepidation that ran through Joseph's mind. Maybe this was the end? Maybe Potiphar had been seething in his anger all this time and now wanted Joseph's head? Was this his death sentence? Have you ever had those moments where it seemed like it was the end? With more force than ten raging men, they snatched up Joseph and hauled him off to the shower to clean him up.

Puzzled by this, Joseph asks what was going on, and they inform him that Pharaoh wanted to see him. (I would imagine Joseph thought to himself, *"why on earth would Pharaoh want to see me?"*) Pharaoh had a dream the night before and wanted him to interpret it! His life had been spared, but in his mind, he was thinking, *"interpret a dream, huh?"*

As he entered into the room, perched upon his golden throne, Pharaoh, the King of Egypt, clad in his royal apparel.

> *And Pharaoh said unto Joseph, "I have dreamed a dream,*
> *and there is none that can interpret it: and I have heard say*
> *of thee, that thou canst understand a dream to interpret it."*
> — *Genesis 41:15*

Joseph, hearing the words of Pharaoh, asking him to interpret his dreams, is taken aback by the moment. With his head still spinning from the insanity, he haphazardly glances across the room; there, standing on the right side of the throne with Pharaoh's cup in his hand, was the butler. With a subtle smile and wink, that said it all. In a split second, Joseph's mind rushed back to the day and hour that he had interpreted the dreams of the butler and the baker. Joseph recalls telling the butler, ***"remember me."***

The room is silent. Joseph is now standing before Pharaoh. All eyes are fixed on him. He pauses before speaking; this moment is surreal for Joseph.

> *And Joseph answered Pharaoh, saying, "It is not in me:*
> *God shall give Pharaoh an answer of peace."*
> *And Pharaoh said unto Joseph, "In my dream, behold,*
> *I stood upon the bank of the river." "And, behold, there*
> *came up out of the river seven kine, fatfleshed and well*
> *favoured; and they fed in a meadow." "And, behold, seven*
> *other kine came up after them, poor and very ill favoured*
> *and leanfleshed, such as I never saw in all the land of Egypt*
> *for badness:" "And the lean and the ill favoured kine did eat*
> *up the first seven fat kine:" "And when they had eaten them*
> *up, it could not be known that they had eaten them; but*
> *they were still ill favoured, as at the beginning. So I awoke."*

"And I saw in my dream, and, behold, seven ears came up in one stalk, full and good:" "And, behold, seven ears, withered, thin, and blasted with the east wind, sprung up after them:" "And the thin ears devoured the seven good ears: and I told this unto the magicians; but there was none that could declare it to me."

– Genesis 41:16-24

As Pharaoh began to tell Joseph his dream, I believe calmness descended upon Joseph from the Lord. The nervousness had dissipated. No longer was his guts churning; a still had settled in. Joseph was sure God was going to give him the answer to Pharaoh's dream.

And Joseph said unto Pharaoh, "The dream of Pharaoh is one: God hath shewed Pharaoh what he is about to do." "The seven good kine are seven years; and the seven good ears are seven years: the dream is one." "And the seven thin and ill favoured kine that came up after them are seven years; and the seven empty ears blasted with the east wind shall be seven years of famine." "This is the thing which I have spoken unto Pharaoh: What God is about to do he sheweth unto Pharaoh." "Behold, there come seven years of great plenty throughout all the land of Egypt:" "And there shall arise after them seven years of famine; and all the plenty shall be forgotten in the land of Egypt; and the famine shall consume the land;

"And the plenty shall not be known in the land by reason of that famine following; for it shall be very grievous." "And for that the dream was doubled unto Pharaoh twice; it is because the thing is established by God, and God will shortly

bring it to pass. "Now therefore let Pharaoh look out a man discreet and wise, and set him over the land of Egypt."
— *Genesis 41:25-33*

After Joseph had finished speaking, Pharaoh remained silent for what seemed like an eternity. Not only had Joseph interpreted Pharaoh's dream, but he also revealed Egypt was facing a grim future. The butler, Pharaoh's servants, and all others present stood stiff like statues, utterly motionless except for their eyes, oscillating back and forth from Pharaoh to Joseph. Joseph didn't expect what would happen next. Never in his wildest dreams could Joseph fathom nor comprehend *the change of season* about to occur in his life. Your day is coming too, and it started when you decided to *unplug.*

FROM THE PRISON TO THE PALACE, FROM POVERTY TO PROSPERITY, FROM A PRISONER, TO VICE PRESIDENT

And Pharaoh said unto his servants, "Can we find such a one as this is, a man in whom the Spirit of God is? And Pharaoh said unto Joseph." And Pharaoh said, "Forasmuch as God hath shewed thee all this, there is none so discreet and wise as thou art:" "Thou shalt be over my house, and according unto thy word shall all my people be ruled: only in the throne will I be greater than thou." And Pharaoh said, "I have set thee over all the land of Egypt."
— *Genesis 41:38-41*

Joseph stood there in complete shock at these words. Dumbfounded, Joseph stood mute. He was numb. Beads of sweat began to trickle down his forehead, onto his brow, and gracing his temples --all eyes were set on him. Joseph couldn't believe his ears, nor could the servants of Pharaoh.

Bowing his head with his eyes closed and ever so slightly shaking it in disbelief, Joseph, was utterly beside himself.

Pharaoh called for his servants, and the next thing he knew, Joseph was being rushed off to his new suite, where royal apparel would be waiting for him. The celebration would begin shortly, as Pharaoh had also prepared Joseph's second chariot to ride in. They paraded throughout Egypt's streets, proclaiming Joseph as the new ruler and commanded everyone to bow their knee to him. Pharaoh's words echoed in Joseph's mind, *"Only in the throne will I be greater"* (Genesis 41:40).

The nightmare had finally come to an end. No longer would Joseph ever be a slave or a prisoner. Was this a dream? Was this really happening? Tears began to stream down Joseph's face. Just a few hours ago, Joseph was cleaning out prison cells and preparing for daily tasks that had become his way of life since being imprisoned. He thought about his father and his brothers if they could only see him now. God had given him the interpretation of Pharaoh's dream, complete control over Egypt, and even rule over Pharaoh's house. That evening, as Joseph retired to his royal suite, he stopped to look at his reflection in the mirror just before changing into his evening wear. Astonished, Joseph could not believe his eyes. Rubbing his hands across the smooth silk robe that covered his body, a far cry from his burlap prison garb. Joseph was a free man. His *change of season* had come.

> *And Joseph was thirty years old when he stood before Pharaoh king of Egypt. And Joseph went out from the presence of Pharaoh, and went throughout all the land of Egypt.*
> *– Genesis 41:46*

The jagged wounds from the past would begin to heal. The pain of betrayal from his brother's as he watched them fade in the distance, shackled on a wagon-train destined to Egypt, would begin to diminish.

Once surrounded by strangers to be sold off as a slave, Joseph would now have the entire kingdom at his command.

From the time Joseph was sold by his brothers until he stood before Pharaoh, it had been thirteen years. In those thirteen years, God was preparing him for that one day. I don't know how long your season will be. One thing I do know is, God is not unrighteous, and He will never leave or forsake you; He will bring you out!

In those solitary moments, I believe Joseph asked the same questions you asked yourself, *"God, why am I here…What did I do to deserve this…Why me…What's this all about…When is this going to end…. Will I ever see the light at the end of the tunnel?"* Personally, I've asked myself and God those very questions in my darkest times. I've wanted to believe that all things work together for good, to them that love God, even when it seems like you feel entirely forsaken.

Joseph's answer to those questions of *"why"* wouldn't come until years down the road, when the very ones who betrayed him, and sold him, would be the ones whose lives Joseph would save. You may not get all your answers at once. Neither did Joseph. God gave him pieces of the puzzle, little by little, because God was still preparing him and *"unplugging Joseph, from the betrayal of his past."*

In reality, sometimes you have to go through hell before you can get to heaven. You have to bear your cross before you can have your crown. Sometimes we forget that it rains on the just and the unjust. It's easy to get angry at God when you're on a wagon-train headed for Egypt after you've been sold out by the ones you love. It's in these moments you can lose your spiritual bearings and go off course. Faith can become compromised by pain. Weariness can take its toll. Anger, bitterness, and resentment can begin to seep in. Joseph spent years in prison. Undoubtedly, he had his moments, just like you have yours. Remember, *"Weeping may endure for a night but joy cometh in the morning."*

When reading the account of Joseph's exoneration, you are completely enamored. In one day, his life was completely flipped upside down again, only this time for the good. One day he was sold as a slave, and in one day, he became a ruler of a nation. God makes the difference in a day.

> "Until the time that his word came, the word of the LORD tried him."
>
> — Psalms 105:1

The Psalmist writing about Joseph gives you insight into his struggles. He faced believing God when it looked bleak (we've all had those moments). God will test you like He did Joseph. Time is not an uncommon practice God will use to show a man where his faith rests in Him. Abraham faced the test of time when he waited twenty-five years for the promise of God to come to pass in his life. Your test is the test of time.

There's an old saying that says – "Can it stand the test of time?" This phrase refers to the ability to last beyond what most expect. People expect you to fail, quit, and buckle under pressure. They don't think you'll stand the test of time in your walk with the Lord. People thought I was going to quit serving God when my daughter died. It was a low point in my life; God didn't fail me. Life happens, and faith is rugged. You're a fighter, not a quitter. You won't give up, and you won't back down. You are more than a conqueror in Christ.

Faithfulness in those dark periods of your life will be the inspiration and strength for others to glean from. The prison cell was a place of preparation for Joseph. The pain of being ripped away from his family was the strengthening he needed to have faith in God. Your prison cell, whatever it may be, is the place of preparation. Your pain is building your strength, and through your weakness, you will be made stronger.

"For God is not unrighteous to forget your work and labour of love, which ye have shewed toward his name" (Hebrews 6:10). It's in the trial of time that you think God has forgotten you, but in reality, it's the beginning of your *change of season!* God hasn't forgotten you; He's preparing you. One of my favorite verses of scripture can be found in Romans; Paul is writing about Abraham's tenacity and his unwavering faith in his trial of time.

> *"And being not weak in faith, he considered not his own*
> *body now dead, when he was about an hundred years old,*
> *neither yet the deadness of Sara's womb: He staggered not at*
> *the promise of God through unbelief; but was strong in faith,*
> *giving glory to God; And being fully persuaded that, what he*
> *had promised, he was able also to perform."*
> *– Romans 4:19-21*

You must come to grips with yourself and your faith; too many times, you consider your situations and circumstance more than God. Not only is Abraham the father of the faith, but he's also the father of time, spiritually speaking. The likelihood of Abraham and Sarah having a child at that point in their life seemed utterly impossible. In your mind, you tell yourself, the probability of the promises of God coming to pass in your life seems impossible. It happens for others, but it never seems to happen for me.

For twenty-five years, Abraham waited for God to perform what seemed impossible as he wandered from place to place following the Will of God, waiting for the promise of God. It was the test of time. Pastor W. J. Davidson preached a message entitled *"out of nowhere,"* and that's precisely what happened to Abraham; and that's precisely what's going to happen to you. *"Out of nowhere,"* God's going to show up.

> *And the LORD appeared unto him in the plains of*
> *Mamre: and he sat in the tent door in the heat of the day.*
> *And they said unto him, "Where is Sarah thy wife?" And*
> *he said, "Behold, in the tent." And he said, "I will certainly*

return unto thee according to the time of life; and, lo, Sarah thy wife shall have a son." And Sarah heard it in the tent door, which was behind him. Now Abraham and Sarah were old and well stricken in age; and it ceased to be with Sarah after the manner of women. Therefore Sarah laughed within herself, saying, "After I am waxed old shall I have pleasure, my lord being old also?" And the LORD said unto Abraham, "Wherefore did Sarah laugh, saying, Shall I of a surety bear a child, which am old?" "Is anything too hard for the LORD? At the time appointed I will return unto thee, according to the time of life, and Sarah shall have a son."

– Genesis 18:1, 9-14

Just like that, out of nowhere, God shows up when you least expect Him. Abraham may not have been expecting a house call that day, but he was waiting for the house call in his spirit every day. You have to walk in the place of expectation. You have to live like you're waiting for a "house call." You can't let doubt creep in and drain your faith in God's Word. You have to speak His Word and His Promises in your life. Yes, it becomes difficult at times, and discouragement tries to seep in, but get ready because that's usually the time when God shows up to pay you a house call.

Twenty-five years is a long time in your mind to wait for something --it's called the test of time. Abraham was one hundred years old before the promise came. At the age of seventy-five, God called him out with only a promise of an unseen son. God has called you out with the unseen blessing of eternal life and His blessings in the tangible of this life. Both are unseen at first, but as you grow in faith and believe God's Word, they become more evident. Live like you're waiting for the knock at the door, Joseph did, because out of nowhere is when God shows up, and *"Changes Your Season."*

CHAPTER 8

"UNPLUGGED OR NOT UNPLUGGED?"

Hopefully, you are now starting to identify within yourself and the things you are *"plugged"* into and reconciling them. The true measure of a person is not known until they are tested to see if, in fact, they are u*nplugged* or not. When confronted and faced with the past, the results reveal whatever it is that haunts them.

As you see with Joseph, life had taken on new meaning. He was *unplugged* from his prison, and Egypt never looked better. Joseph felt like God had set him free, enjoying the fineries of what wealth and power can afford. I have seen one inherent trait in humanity, and I venture to speculate it was in Joseph. Money and power can anesthetize the pain. Anger and sadness feel like they have been alleviated when replaced by the false comfort of gain. Joseph immersed himself in anything and everything that was Egypt, burying his past. Joseph would name his firstborn son Manasseh, which means, *"God hath made me forget all my toil and my father's house."*

Joseph's diplomacy with commercial trade and the distribution of goods and services would be critical in preserving Egypt during the famine. The seven years of plenty had ended, and the seven years of famine had set in. By the droves, nations began to pour into Egypt's harbors, desperately seeking relief from the famine for their hungry families. The Nile River looked like a modern-day traffic jam at rush hour. Chaos had broken out globally as food shortages were now everywhere, and word had gotten out that Egypt had a treasure trove of provision.

> *Now when Jacob saw that there was corn in Egypt, Jacob said unto his sons, "Why do ye look one upon another?" And he said, 'Behold, I have heard that there is corn in Egypt: get you down thither, and buy for us from thence; that we may live, and not die." And Joseph's ten brethren went down to buy corn in Egypt. But Benjamin, Joseph's brother, Jacob sent not with his brethren; for he said, "Lest peradventure mischief befall him."*
>
> *— Genesis 42:1-4*

When you least expect it, God will send you a reminder. Not only you but those who have betrayed you. Why? Because He has to show you whether you're *unplugged* or not. Seven years of reprieve, growing and excelling in his political office, a wife, and children, made it easy to block out and ignore the past. Mark it down. Life will come full circle, and when it does, it shows you what you are made of.

> *And Joseph was the governor over the land, and he it was that sold to all the people of the land: and Joseph's brethren came, and bowed down themselves before him with their faces to the earth. And Joseph saw his brethren, and he knew them, but made himself strange unto them, and spake roughly unto them; and he said unto them, "Whence come ye? And they said, "From the land of Canaan to buy food." And Joseph knew his brethren, but they knew not him. And Joseph remembered the dreams which he dreamed of them!*
>
> *— Genesis 42:6-9*

Being a Christian at times can be trying, especially when you want vengeance on your foes. You want them to feel what you felt when they hurt you. Not only did Joseph remember his dreams, but also his pain. The time had come to see if Joseph was *unplugged or not unplugged?* Not only was it a test for Joseph, but it was also a test for his brothers to see if they had really changed their ways. Joseph had named his firstborn son Manasseh, meaning, *"God hath made me forget all my toil and my father's house."* But, did Joseph really forget all the toils of his father's house?

Christianity is tested; the critical moment when you think that you've overcome and *unplugged* from the offense, only to find out if you have or haven't, is when God presents a before your face. Had his brothers changed? Were they genuinely sorry for what they had done to Joseph? The testing process begins, Joseph will not only test his brothers, but God will test Joseph. God is going to test you, not because He's being cruel and wants to remind you of the pain, but to help you get the victory once and for all. God shows you whether you're *unplugged* or not.

Reading in David's writings (Psalms) many times, you see David wanting God's wrath to fall on his enemies and those that opposed him.

> *"Break their teeth, O God, in their mouth: break out the great teeth of the young lions, O LORD." "Let them melt away as waters which run continually: when he bendeth his bow to shoot his arrows, let them be as cut in pieces."*
> *— Psalms 58:6-7*

Wrath is cruel, and anger destroys, and there are probably not too many Christians who haven't felt the same way at some point in their life. There isn't a more remarkable example of overcoming evil with good than the Lord Jesus Christ! Under the Old Testament Law, a man was only judged for his external actions; he never had to account for his thoughts nor his evil conjecture. However, through Jeremiah, God did say, *"the heart is deceitful above all things, and desperately wicked" (Jeremiah 17:9),* but man was never sentenced for it.

A man was only judged on taste not, touch not, etc. The Ten Commandments are strictly natural commandments that deal with natural actions; howbeit his actions directly reflect the inner man. God does not address that in the Old Testament like He did in the New Testament. In the Perfect Law of Liberty, Jesus describes in detail what He expects from you and me as His disciples. Christ does not leave one stone unturned. He goes above the natural law and delves into the Spiritual Law. Christ reveals what the real purpose of the Old Testament Law was. Jesus first gives you the natural Law. Then He gives you the Spiritual Law, "The Perfect Law of Liberty."

> *"Ye have heard that it hath been said, An eye for an eye, and a tooth for a tooth." (O.T. Law) "But I say unto you, That ye resist not evil: but whosoever shall smite thee on thy right cheek, turn to him the other also." (N.T. Perfect Law of Liberty)*
>
> *"Ye have heard that it hath been said, Thou shalt love thy neighbor, and hate thine enemy." (O.T Law) "But I say unto you, Love your enemies, bless them that curse you, do good to them that hate you, and pray for them which despitefully use you, and persecute you." (N.T. Perfect Law of Liberty)*
> *— Matthew 5:38-39, 43-44*

The moment of truth had arrived. It had been over twenty years since Joseph had last seen his brothers, and the images of their hatred, mockery, and betrayal by selling him into slavery were burned into Joseph's mind. The smug look on their faces, as they gladly received the money from the slave traders. Joseph remembered as he watched them turned their backs on him as he cried for them to help him, but they wouldn't. Now twenty-plus years later, the dreams have come to pass, and they were bowing at his feet. Reciting his dreams of their sheaves bowing to his sheaves, the sun, and the moon, it was overwhelming. Joseph now holds the upper hand. Over twenty years of hurts and soul searching, trying to find reasoning why his life had become what it had? He had to go to prison for a crime he didn't commit --only to become a prince in Egypt. There standing before him were the perpetrators of his pain, making Joseph aware that his wound hadn't completely healed just yet.

> *And Joseph said unto them, "Ye are spies; to see the na-kedness of the land ye are come." And they said unto him, "Nay, my lord, but to buy food are thy servants come." "We are all one man's sons; we are true men, thy servants are no spies." And he said unto them, "Nay, but to see the nakedness of the land ye are come." And they said, "Thy servants are twelve brethren, the sons of one man in the land of Canaan; and, behold, the youngest is this day with our father, and one is not."*
>
> *– Genesis 42:9-13*

I would imagine seeing them stand there and lie to his face and state, *"one is not,"* implying Joseph was dead infuriated him. *"One is not, only because you sold him off to the slave traders,"* ran through Joseph's mind as a wave of mixed emotion deluged him. It seemed like nothing had changed. They were still up to their evil ways. It was almost as if their dialogue was premeditated. Why didn't they just say we are the sons of one man and eleven brethren? Why did they have to say twelve? It had been over twenty years since they sold Joseph.

> *And Joseph said unto them, "That is it that I spake unto you, saying, Ye are spies." "Hereby ye shall be proved: By the life of Pharaoh ye shall not go forth hence, except your*

youngest brother come hither." "Send one of you, and let him
fetch your brother, and ye shall be kept in prison, that your
words may be proved, whether there be any truth in you: or
else by the life of Pharaoh surely ye are spies." And he put
them all together into ward three days.

— Genesis 42:14-17

Not only were Joseph's brothers in prison for three days, but Joseph was too. The feelings and emotions from his past began to resurface, and Joseph realized he was still *"plugged"* into them. It had been over twenty years, and during those three days, God begins to deal with Joseph. God starts opening up to Joseph His Will. In Joseph's mind, God begins to answer some of the questions he asked during his time of incarceration. Joseph starts to understand his dreams more clearly now, and God's plan for his life is becoming lucent.

Let the Lord minister to you His mercy, as His Will becomes more transparent, in your mind and spirit, like it did to Joseph. God is not a God of waste, nor does He do anything without a purpose. There is a purpose for your pain.

And Joseph said unto them the third day, "This do,
and live; for I fear God:" "If ye be true men, let one of your
brethren be bound in the house of your prison: go ye, carry
corn for the famine of your houses:" "But bring your youngest
brother unto me; so shall your words be verified, and ye shall
not die. And they did so."

— Genesis 42:18-20

Then the unexpected happened. What would transpire next would be the very thing that would start the healing process in Joseph's heart towards his brothers. Sometimes healing comes in ways you never thought imaginable. Sometimes it comes from those who caused all the pain in the first place. Up until this point, Joseph had only spoken to his brothers through an interpreter, never revealing that he spoke Hebrew.

> And they said one to another," We are verily guilty concerning our brother, in that we saw the anguish of his soul, when he besought us, and we would not hear; therefore is this distress come upon us." And Reuben answered them, saying, "Spake I not unto you, saying, Do not sin against the child; and ye would not hear? therefore, behold, also his blood is required." And they knew not that Joseph understood them; for he spake unto them by an interpreter.
>
> – Genesis 42:21-23

Their voice inflections and crestfallen expressions told Joseph a different story, one he never heard before. They were living with the guilt and sins of their past. They were tormented and plagued for betraying their brother. Joseph's twenty years of wondering if they ever had remorse for their actions was finally answered. Yes, they were sorry and felt ashamed for their actions towards him. The tone in their voices said it all. For over twenty years, Joseph's brothers lived with regret and condemnation for the crimes they committed against him, and it had haunted them like Joseph's pain haunted him. Unable to contain his emotions, *Joseph turned himself about from them, and wept (Genesis 42:24).*

Knowing that this was only the beginning of the famine and that there were still years to come, Joseph devises a plan. He longed to see his brother Benjamin and to feel his father's embrace, so he had to ensure that they would return to Egypt, *"Joseph took from them Simeon and bound him before their eyes" (Genesis 42:24).*

The laws of sowing and reaping had come to pass. The trapped and helpless feeling Joseph felt when they sold him, his brothers were now crippled with. Unable to say a word or plead with the Lord of Egypt, they held their peace. They stood mute and looked on as Simeon disappear from their sight, so reminiscent of the day, they watched Joseph disappear from theirs when they sold him.

> *Then Joseph commanded to fill their sacks with corn, and*
> *to restore every man's money into his sack, and to give them*
> *provision for the way: and thus did he unto them. And they*
> *laded their asses with the corn, and departed thence.*
> — *Genesis 42:25-26*

At first, it was silent as they made their departure from Egypt. No one spoke a word. The only sound you could hear was the sound of the asses hooves striking the ground. Laden with provisions to sustain the family and their past guilt, Jacob's sons were beleaguered. How would they explain to their father Simeon's fate and how the Lord of Egypt demanded Benjamin's return with them if they ever wanted food again? Their sin against Joseph and the wickedness of their treachery had come back on them.

It had been over twenty years since their assault on Joseph, and the timing of the Lord's vengeance is not always the same as ours. You can mark it down. The Lord will repay those who wrong His children. Life had come full circle for Joseph's brothers. All of their emotions from the past were now present. They dreaded to see the look on Jacob's face when they would tell him of Simeon's imprisonment, knowing it would resurface the pain they witnessed when they told him of Joseph; only this time, it wouldn't be a lie. The mental anguish of seeing the hurt in their father again would be unbearable. Knowing for over twenty years, they had concealed their lie concerning Joseph's death, as they had to watch Jacob mourn his loss for years, now they would have to reopen the same wound of loss again. Would Jacob let them take Benjamin with them, or would they starve? All these thoughts swirled through their conversation on the way back to Canaan. However, the torment wasn't over. Joseph had another surprise waiting for them. Knowing the journey back to Canaan would be lengthy, and at some point, they would have to feed and water their animals, a surprise would be awaiting them. The Law of reaping and sowing is not a respecter of a person to any degree. God's Word cannot lie. No one is exempt, as seen in the lives of the patriarchs of your faith.

> *And as one of them opened his sack to give his ass proven-*
> *der in the inn, he espied his money; for, behold, it was in his*
> *sack's mouth. And he said unto his brethren, "My money is*
> *restored; and, lo, it is even in my sack: and their heart failed*
> *them, and they were afraid, saying one to another, What is*
> *this that God hath done unto us?"*
>
> *– Genesis 42:27-28*

I'll say one thing about the sons of Jacob; despite their pernicious ways, they still bear some resemblance of respect, and acknowledgment for God, in their lives. Knowing the evil of their past and that no one is exempt, they question their Deity's actions – *"what is this that God hath done unto us"*? Not only did Joseph strip them of their will, but he also gave them a taste of their own medicine and made them feel helpless and fearing the wrath of God.

There are times in life where you have done your wrongs, and now you must face the music. Life comes full circle, and accepting responsibility for your actions, is one of the first steps to *"unplugging."* By doing so, it will begin the healing process for those you have hurt. When Joseph saw and heard them remorseful for what they had done to him, something changed inside him. God's plan became even more apparent.

When everything was turned upside down and inside out during Joseph's life, God didn't appear to be anywhere in sight. As Joseph stood in the courtroom being falsely accused of attempted rape and sent to prison, God's Will for his life looked like nothing but a murky, chaotic mess. Amid your darkest trials, God's plan for your life is the furthest thing from clear. Don't give up! Hold on; answers are just around the corner. If God called you to it, He will bring you through it. I promise you God will show you the light at the end of the tunnel; it's a promise in His Word.

God is the most excellent multi-tasker on the planet, even when we can't see it. You're never alone in your trial. As you read the narrative in the lives of these men and its tangled thread, God's hand was in all of it. From Jacob and his sons, the butler, the baker, Potiphar, Pharoah, and a famine, God was working behind the scenes at the same time He was creating them. God is dealing with everyone in your trial at the same time He's dealing with you. People that you don't even realize are being dealt with, God is talking to. What a majestic God we serve.

Jacob's faith would also be tested by God to see if he really trusted in Him. The Apostle Peter wrote, *"Beloved, think it not strange concerning the fiery trial, which is to try you."* Trials are a measuring stick of your trust in God and the building blocks of your faith.

As his sons recalled the events that transpired with the Lord of Egypt and the imprisonment of Simeon, Jacob is crushed. Adding insult to injury, Jacob's words drive the dagger deeper into the souls of his ashamed sons, *"My son shall not go down with you; for his brother is dead, and he is left alone: if mischief befall him by the way in the which ye go, then shall ye bring down my gray hairs with sorrow to the grave."* (Genesis 42:38)

> *And the famine was sore in the land. And it came to pass,*
> *when they had eaten up the corn which they had brought*
> *out of Egypt, their father said unto them, "Go again, buy*
> *us a little food." And Judah spike unto him, saying, "The*
> *man did solemnly protest unto us, saying, Ye shall not see my*

face, except your brother be with you." "If thou wilt send our brother with us, we will go down and buy thee food."

— Genesis 43:1-3

Backed into a corner with nowhere to go, Jacob is forced to acquiesce and relinquish Benjamin. The mandate from the Lord of Egypt was, *"no, Benjamin, no food."* It was imperative for the tribe's survival that Benjamin goes with his brothers back to Egypt. Israel is desperate to hang on, finding himself in an uncomfortable position in life. All the tribe's provisions have been depleted, and they have no other options. Jacob is once again in a wrestling match, only this time it's with his heart.

These are the places that God has to take us to, to show us if we are *"unplugged"* or not. This is the *"fiery trial"* that Peter spoke of. You can pray the prayer of faith, you can claim healing for your best friend, and you can shout for joy on the mountain-top, but in the valley, can you trust God? Can you trust God when He calls for the only thing you've got left and don't want to let it go? Will you trust Him?

Since the death of Rachel and the loss of Joseph, Benjamin was the only thing Jacob had left to hold on to of Rachel. Jacob's faith was on trial. Your faith will be put on trial, at various points, in your life. You will stand in the courtroom of the Almighty God.

Jacob had no counsel; he had no representation to defend him. The prosecutor was Jacob's mind, and his key witnesses were his past, coupled with his fears. The cross-examination was grueling. Many emotions testified against him, Jacob's own words ran through his mind, *"All These Things Are Against Me."* Capitalizing on his failures as a person and father. These are the crossroads in life that we arrive at in times of direr straights!

Feeling like Jacob, you're backed in a corner with nowhere to go, and the only option seems to be the one that is the most feared; welcome to the courtroom of the Almighty God. Confronted with your past and the fear of the present, you stand before the Judge of the whole earth. Like

Jacob, you're now in a wrestling match with your heart. You are faced with having to give something up that you love for the sake of others. When Jesus told you to take up your *"cross,"* He never promised that it wouldn't be heavy. Jacob's cross was giving up Benjamin, what's yours? Are you willing to relinquish and acquiesce to the mandate of the Lord?

> *And Judah said unto Israel his father, "Send the lad with me, and we will arise and go; that we may live, and not die, both we, and thou, and also our little ones."*
> *"I will be surety for him; of my hand shalt thou require him: if I bring him not unto thee, and set him before thee, then let me bear the blame for ever."*
> *— Genesis 43:8-9*

> *And their father Israel said unto them, "If it must be so now, do this; take of the best fruits in the land in your vessels, and carry down the man a present, a little balm, and a little honey, spices, and myrrh, nuts, and almonds."*
> *"And take double money in your hand; and the money that was brought again in the mouth of your sacks, carry it again in your hand; peradventure it was an oversight:" "Take also your brother, and arise, go again unto the man." "And God Almighty give you mercy before the man, that he may send away your other brother, and Benjamin. If I be bereaved of my children, I am bereaved."*
> *— Genesis 43:11-14*

With only two options, starvation or Benjamin, Jacob submits his will. He releases Benjamin to Judah's care, who assures his father that he will take personal responsibility and bear the blame forever if something should happen to Benjamin. Sometimes God forces your hand and puts you in the position Jacob was in. Why? Because, in order for you to *unplug,* sometimes it means giving up Benjamin when it feels like, *"All These Things Are Against Me."*

These are the Benjamin moments in your walk with the Lord; it's where the mountain standing before you is seemingly insurmountable. The meal in the barrel is only but a handful, and there's nothing in sight to replace it, and God tells you to give it away. At the end of the month, there's more month than money, and the church takes up an offering. The overwhelming feeling of utter hopelessness has you in its throes of *"All These Things Are Against Me!"*

As Jacob watches his sons ride off to Egypt with Benjamin, the patriarch is broken. Jacob is standing there, fragmented and the helpless feeling of vulnerability and being completely out of control engulfed the aged man. Jacob's mind begins to playback past events in his life. He reflects on the milestones and the watermarks. *The Dream Of The Ladder At Bethel…..The Vows That He Vowed To God At Bethel…..The Wrestling Match With God At Penuel…..The Name Change…..The Crippling.*

What did this all mean? Would Jacob ever see Benjamin or Simeon again? All these things seemed to be against him. The correlation between Jacob and you is genuine. In your walk with the Lord, there are the times and seasons where His promises seem to fade away into obscurity, blocked out by the overshadowing dark clouds of trials and tribulation that can leave you feeling destitute and forsaken. You become jaded in your spirit as you see yourself standing in the shoes of the shattered old man Jacob, a man with the calling of God on his life, and yet it appears he has been abandoned by Him.

As I'm writing this portion of the book, I can't help but look retrospectively into the things that have transpired over my twenty-plus years of serving the Lord. I can say with surety, I've had those Jacob moments in my life. I know the overwhelming feelings of utter hopelessness and despair. I know what it's like to experience, the emotions of every wall surrounding me imploding. Every front seemed to be a losing battle, wondering where God was in my situation? Did the God that says He knows, sees, and hears all, really understand what was going on in my life? I got angry at the Lord, and rage engulfed me in my moments of despair. I had feelings of doubt, wondering why and how come I questioned Him and His Word. These are the feelings and emotions that grip you in the cross-examination process in your trial.

The crestfallen Jacob watched as his sons disappeared from his sight. As the days passed, the old man could not keep himself from being captive by his thoughts --Jacob's mind was his purgatory. Had they made it safely to Egypt? Was Simeon dead or alive? Had Benjamin been taken captive too and put in prison? Were they on their way home already? Throughout the day, the old man would look in Egypt's direction, hoping and praying to see his son's images on the horizon, only to be disappointed. It's in these critical moments of life, like Jacob, where you find out if you are *"unplugged"* or *not?* In the testing phase, it's through the manifestation of a trial that you see where your faith rests in the Lord.

> *"Examine yourselves, to see whether you are holding to your faith. Test yourselves. Do you not realize that Jesus Christ is in you? - unless indeed you fail to meet the test."*
> *— 2 Corinthians 13:5 RSV*

The Apostle Paul wrote: *"Examine yourselves, to see whether you are holding to your faith. Test yourselves"* (2 Corinthians 13:5 ESV). There is the necessity for self-examination. Education is only what you retain. Passing or failing your exams reveals whether you have been paying attention and comprehending the information presented to you? So operates faith. Faith is an education that is progressively gained. Faith increases as the knowledge of God's Word is sown into your heart. Faith increases by hearing the Word of God preached. Trials and tribulations are your tests of comprehension. It is in the tested and tried, trice moments, where your believability in the Word of God, through faith, is either passed or failed. Your faith must stand trial to see if you are *"Unplugged"* or *"Not?"*

> *"Count it all joy, my brethren, when you meet various trials, for you know that the testing of your faith produces steadfastness." "And let steadfastness have its full effect, that you may be perfect and complete, lacking in nothing."*
> *– James 1:2-4 RSV*

CHAPTER 9

FULL CIRCLE

It was the summer of 1986, my father and I had just returned from a jaunty vacation of waterskiing, fishing, and wakeboarding at my grandparent's waterfront property in Oscoda, Michigan. It was a Monday, the sun was out, the birds were singing in harmony, and the flowers were in bloom; it was a beautiful Michigan summer day. For me, on this gorgeous day, the business at hand was cutting the grass, per my father's request. Being the lazy sixteen-year-old punk that I was, I managed to muster up enough ambition to walk out to the shed and extract the lawnmower from its resting place. *(I was still contemplating if I was going to cut the grass or not. I figured if I at least opened the shed and got it out, this could in some way help my decision).* Haphazardly scanning the contents that encompassed the lawnmower in its wooden mansion, I spotted something that immediately captivated my attention. There, perched upon the top shelf, sitting amongst the other occupants, were two brand new aerosol cans of black spray paint. My curiosity was peaked, so I reached up and took them down from their resting place. Puzzled as to why they were there and how on earth I had never noticed them before, I carefully examined them. After the examination was complete, and I could not determine the reasoning for them being there, I returned them to the void on the shelf where they once stood. I embraced the lawnmower and commenced cutting the lawn.

You didn't have electric starters on lawnmowers in those days, and there were no self-propelled ones either. If you wanted the grass cut, you had to push it, and it was a workout.

As fate would have it, my best friend in high school *(and still one of my best friends in life)*, Bommer *(James)*, shows up at my house on this day. Bommer, like me, had moved away from our small town in elementary school. I moved to Roseville, MI., and Jim moved to Scottsdale, Arizona. Bommer had a West Coast flair to his game, a strapping young lad and sporting somewhat of a radical skater/surfer look. I, on the other hand, was a rocker. We became best friends that summer, and after that, it was game on. We blended our fashions together and created our own look. Because of the outlandish apparel we sported in high school, the dress code was rewritten *(it was that bad, true story)*.

We were not troublemakers by and large, but we had our fair share of mischief. As the saying goes, "An idle mind is the devil's playground." We were bored, and I got this great idea *(at least at the time, it seemed like a great idea)*. As I returned the lawnmower to its resting place, those aerosol cans jumped out at me. I walked over to the shelf and retrieved them from their station; I turned to Jim without saying a word, just a smile.

Beaming with devilish smirks, it was time to go add a little color to the world. We didn't start on our adventure with any ill intent or a specific target. It wasn't like we hated anybody, or we were seeking revenge for some wrong. We were just going to add a little shade to life. It started off small, just some simple lines on the sidewalk and on the street, here a little and there a little along the way, nothing major. How and why we ended up heading in the school's direction to this day still puzzles me. There was no rhyme or reason to where we were going. We ambled along the way on our journey to nowhere, in particular, painting as we went. We passed a group of guys playing basketball on the campus court. One of the guys was an upper classmate, whom I recently had a quarrel with. Bommer pointed at him and, in a loud voice, for all present to hear, said, *"Look, Teal, there's that punk you slapped around the other day in front of his girlfriend."* In front of all his friends, Jim's insults and embarrassing comments would be the final nail in the coffin by the end of the day.

We rounded the corner and were now in front of the elementary school, making our way past the high school. In between the two structures there, tucked away in a courtyard, was our next target. Standing alone, and chained with no way to escape, shackled to the bike rack, was a ten-speed *(dating myself and all those who know what a ten-speed bike is)*. The bike was in mint condition. Again, it was one of the trice moments where two minds become one, the results of best friends, with the same mindset. Without a word being said, the renovation would soon begin. We approached the helpless victim with a vengeance. The poor thing didn't stand a chance. It was like a lamb gone astray and that had wandered into a pack of wolves. As we approached our prey, we violently shook our paint cans. The sound of the stone, mixing the paint, echoed off the walls in the courtyard. We swooped down on it without mercy like the *Blitzkrieg;* we unleashed our attack. The smell of fresh paint permeated the air, along with the hissing sounds, as our fury was in full effect. With each stroke of the attack, our prey's appearance changed before our eyes. Disfiguring its vesture and wilting from the vicious onslaught, the ten-speed was helpless. As the aerosol-cloud settled, we were satisfied with the custom new look, stepping back to observe our handy work. Our task was finished here, and it was now time to move on.

Making our departure from the courtyard on our special opts, mission, code name, *"adding color to the world."* We headed in the direction of yet a larger canvas with more options to complete our assignment, "the playground." Directly behind the school was the Vlasic Pickle Factory; there was a slight breeze, and the fresh smell of pickles hung in the air. As young artists', our creative minds began to flow and express themselves freely, as the spirit of inspiration moved us.

Off in the distance on the northside of the playground was a group of older guys playing basketball (we didn't recognize any of them). We zeroed in on our next mark, positioned ourselves, and opened fire with our attack's second wave. The unsuspecting had no chance: the slide, swing-set, monkey-bars, and the school's walls, were utterly defenseless. Wave after wave of our aerosol strike left its mark of destruction on their surface; it was a complete frenzy!

Making our way to the West side of the playground, we were ready to unleash our final ambush with cans in hand. I noticed that the group playing basketball was gone. When I looked up again, they were making their charge in our direction. Well, it didn't take Einstein to figure this one out. Yep, you guessed it. The ten-speed bike we custom painted was one of the guys who had been playing basketball. He must have really been surprised when he walked up to the bike rack and seen the custom finish we gave it. Apparently, his taste was different than ours, and he was not happy with its custom finish.

Seeing we were outnumbered, three to one, we ran! The raid was over, and the tides had turned, and now there was a counterattack. We darted off towards the Pickle Factory with the guys in hot pursuit. Fortunately, I had worked there and knew the layout of the grounds. The cucumbers are stored in large vats where they ferment until they are ready to become pickles. The vats are probably ten to twelve feet in circumference and fifteen to eighteen feet tall. There are hundreds of them side by side, only being separated by a few feet of space in between. It's literally a maze. To get to the field of vats, we first had to go through a cemetery. We were jumping and dodging tombstones as we made our way into the maze. Luckily, we had enough of a head start that we lost them in the field of vats, making our way north in the maze.

Gasping for air as our lungs felt like they were going to explode, or should I say implode from oxygen depletion—we ran for our lives. We had successfully eluded our attackers and came out on the factory's Northwest side by the train tracks. Our pursuers were nowhere in sight. Exhausted and as adrenaline surged through our veins, we had narrowly escaped an angry mob seeking vengeance. Making our way towards the train tracks, laughing in jubilation, we were suddenly interrupted and found out that someone had called the police when we saw a cruiser coming down the road in our direction. It wasn't over, and it was still game on.

Once again, we were left with few options. The only one that made real sense was to head down the train tracks, where his car couldn't go. So off and running, we went! After running about a quarter of a mile, we detoured off the tracks and ran into the backyard of a friend's house. We stayed there for a couple of hours, hiding until things cooled down. Needless to say, we each headed home and called it a day.

The next day I went to my Aunt and Uncle's house to visit for a couple of days. When I got back home, my father wasn't too pleased with me. He informed me a day before my return, he got a house call from the local police, telling him that charges were being pressed against me for destruction to city property, along with a friend of mine, James Bommer. Unable to lie my way out of it, I was busted. A court date was set, and I had to go before the judge and faced the charges being brought against me. I admitted my guilt and was sentenced to six months' probation. The judge was very stern and informed me that I could have gone to a juvenile home for my offenses, but instead, I had to meet every two weeks with a probation officer. For the first month or so, I never missed an appointment. After a while, my fear of going to a juvenile home wore off, and I stopped going. I wanted to enjoy the rest of the summer and going to probation was an inconvenience.

I soon found out this is not how the legal system works. You don't stop going to your probation appointments because you think they're a waste of your time and your summer. It wasn't long, the police were back at my house, and another court date was set. Now I was fearful, I knew I had really messed up, and the juvenile home could be my new residence. The day came that I had to go stand before the judge for the second time, and I had come *full circle.* It was a long and quiet ride to the courthouse. At that time, my dad was in the middle of going through his second divorce with my stepmom; he was trying to get custody of my little sister. He told me that my *"reckless and destructive actions"* could prevent him from getting custody of her. This added insult to injury because the last thing I wanted for my little sister was to live with her alcoholic mother. My actions could have portrayed him as an unfit and unstable parent who couldn't control his rebellious teenage son.

We arrived at the courthouse, and that sick, nervous feeling you get in your stomach, when you're about to face the music, had taken a strong foothold in my gut. I knew the judge was not going to be happy with me; I was humbled. When the judge called my name and read my charges, he asked me how I plea, and I told him,

"Guilty, your honor."

He asked me if I understood the charges being brought against me and that there would be punishment for my negligence to obey the law, and I said,

"yes."

He then called me up to his desk and looked me straight in the eyes, and said: *"Listen, if you don't want to obey the law, and you think the law doesn't apply to you, and you can do whatever you want, and you don't have to go to probation, I can make the necessary arrangements for you to be picked up from jail, taken to school, and then after school taken back to jail, do you want me to do that?"*

"No, your honor."

There was a slight pause, then he said: *"The court finds Thomas L. Teal Jr. guilty of the violation of probation, and probation will be extended for an*

additional six more months. No further actions are necessary. I'm sure Thomas
will not be missing any more of his probation appointments, right Thomas?"

"Yes, your honor."

I had been given a second chance. I walked out of that courtroom
with a brand-new attitude and a new respect for the law. I never missed
another appointment.

The same nauseating feeling I had in my stomach as I walked up
those steps to the courthouse to face the judge was the same that Joseph's
brother probably felt. The violation they had done to Joseph had come *full
circle* in their lives, and there was no way to escape it. Everyone felt the
burden, everyone, that is, except for Benjamin; he was still puzzled why
the Lord of Egypt requested his presence?

With the aspirations of trying to gain Joseph's favor, seeing how they
departed not on the greatest terms, they brought Joseph a present. Along
with their money from their previous visit, they brought him an offering
of fruit from the land of Canaan. The sons of Jacob crossed Egypt's threshold, and the silos stood off in the distance; knowing the Lord of Egypt
would be there, the fear of the unknown was overwhelming. Reluctant in
their spirit and trying not to posture their nervousness, they made their
way towards the concierge, where they would check-in and receive their
purchase order. The food lines were as long as the eye could see. The influx
of the masses sojourning was oppressing. Aimlessly they thronged about,
trying to get in line. Immigrants from far and near had come seeking
Egypt's trove of provender. It was hysteria, between the bleating of the
sheep, the mooing of the ox, and the howling of the line director; it was
an orchestra of cacophony.

For hours they stood in line in the sweltering heat, knowing soon
enough they would be face to face with the Lord of Egypt. As they got
closer towards the front of the line, they could see the Lord of Egypt in the
distance. There he was, Zaphnathe-paaneah, delegating rations according
to their purchase orders. As they reached the purchasing agent's desk, they

informed him of what happened with their money being found in their sacks. He obliged them for their honesty but assured them it was not an oversight. He further says, *"it was a blessing from the gods,"* and told them they were next to see the governor. Even in the most challenging situations, honesty is the best policy. It's something God always honors.

FULL CIRCLE

The moment had arrived; they had come *full circle,* and fear of the unknown taunted them. Walking in Joseph's direction, they noticed his eyes made contact with their whereabouts. His gaze fell straight on them, zeroing in on Benjamin. He was utterly transfixed on the younger brother.

> *And when Joseph saw Benjamin with them, he said to the ruler of his house, "Bring these men home, and slay, and make ready; for these men shall dine with me at noon." And the man did as Joseph bade; and the man brought the men into Joseph's house".*
>
> *— Genesis 43:16-17*

When the brothers heard this, they began to fret and wonder what the meaning behind all of this was? Their hearts were filled with fear as they were led away from the silos to Joseph's dining hall. The ambient light from the torches that hung from the walls gave way to their destination, illuminating the passageway and revealing the beauty of their surroundings. They were amazed at the artwork, the gold statues, and the tapestries that decorated the walls encompassing the corridor that led to the dining hall.

> *When Joseph came home, they brought him the present which was in their hand into the house, and bowed themselves to him to the earth.*

– Gen 43:26

This is now the second time that his brothers have bowed themselves to Joseph. He reflected on his dreams, but he was still unsure of his brothers, so he begins an inquiry. He questions them to see in their voice tone, the expressions on their face, and their body language to discern if, in fact, they were *"true men,"* as they claimed. Not only was it a test from Joseph to his brothers, but it was a test for Joseph also.

"Is your father well, the old man of whom ye spake? Is he yet alive?" And they answered, "Thy servant our father is in good health, he is yet alive." And they bowed down their heads and made obeisance.
– Genesis 43:27-28

For the first time in over twenty years, Joseph sees Benjamin, his little brother. There before his eyes stood, the only thing he had in this life that reconnected him to his mother and father, Benjamin. The similarities were incredible, the features, the skin complexion, the hair, and eye color. It was almost as if his mother was standing there before him. It had been over twenty years since Joseph had seen him, and it was such a vivid reminder of her. Joseph's emotions begin to swell as he stared at Benjamin.

And he lifted up his eyes, and saw his brother Benjamin, his mother's son, and said, "Is this your younger brother, of whom ye spake unto me?" And he said, "God be gracious unto thee, my son." And Joseph made haste; for his bowels did yearn upon his brother: and he sought where to weep; and he entered into his chamber and wept there".
– Genesis 43:29-30

The last time Joseph seen Benjamin, he was a little boy when Joseph had been sold off. Over twenty years had passed, and Benjamin had now become a young man. Joseph's heart ached as a flood of childhood memories rushed through him. Benjamin was the only connection he had to their mother, whom he loved, and Jacob, the father he missed. The anger begins to resurface in Joseph towards his brothers; for the years, they robbed him from his family because of their cruel and jealous ways. Joseph had come *full circle,* and the *test begins.*

There is no golden ticket to Heaven. You are going to be tried. If you want to receive a crown of glory, you will come *full circle* in your life at various times when you are confronted with the past. You will be tested to see where your faith truly lies. These are the watermarks and notches in your spiritual staff. These tests are the proving grounds of your faith and your forgiveness. It's where the rubber meets the road, or in the spiritual sense, it's where the Word meets the flesh.

The echoes of their mockery for his dreams and their cruel slurs all reemerge. Joseph internally interrogates his brothers with questions. *"Were you cruel to Benjamin like you were to me…did you make fun of him like you did me… …did you hate Benjamin like you hated me… did Benjamin have any dreams, and did you laughed at him like you laughed at me"*?

It's in these moments when those who have caused much pain in life are standing before you that the test truly begins. The perpetrator of your pain is at your mercy, and the roles have reversed. You hold the upper hand. What are you going to do? It's here where you begin to see if you have genuinely *unplugged* or not?

Do you hold onto the resentments and allow them to keep you in a purgatory of bitterness and seething in anger? Will you unleash your wrath? Has the sinister side of you been waiting for this moment to arrive? What will you do? Your hour of reprisal has come; it's a test. Jesus said, *"Love your enemies, bless them that curse you, do good to them that hate you, and pray for them which despitefully use you and persecute you"* (Matthew

5:44). These are some pretty strong words of advice from the Lord, and His life manifested those very deeds when He allowed man to hang Him on a Cross. At times this is much easier said than done.

Joseph devises a plan because he is still unsure if they are genuinely sorry for what they had done. Uncertain of his own feelings, he will prove their repentance. He continues to play mind games with his guilty betrayers. Dinner is served, and the test begins. Waiting to see their response, Joseph purposely arranged their seating by age. *And they sat before him, the firstborn according to his birthright, and the youngest according to his youth: and the men marveled one at another (Genesis 43:33).* The brothers were amazed. How on earth did he know the birth order of them? It was evident that Benjamin was the youngest; his face didn't bear the weathered image of his much older brothers, but to differentiate Judah from Dan, Reuben from Asher, baffled them. Besides the fact, they couldn't even have a conversation with him except through an interpreter. They were shepherds, and shepherds were an abomination to the Egyptians. The servants of Joseph and Joseph sat apart from them. Egyptian tradition says, if you eat bread with a Shepherd, it is an abomination; it was forbidden to dine at the same table *(Genesis 43:32).*

Joseph observes and watches his brother's reaction; their countenance tells a story that they are somewhat shaken by the seating arrangement. Dinner is served, and when the portions are delved out, Benjamin's portion is five times greater than his brothers. Looking at one another with amazement, yet no one says a word, and Joseph looks on. They enjoy themselves eating and drinking the most exquisite food Egypt had to offer. In the distance, as Joseph watches his betrayers indulge, he's haunted by Reuben's confession: *"Spake I not unto you, saying, Do not sin against the child; and ye would not hear? therefore, behold, also his blood is required"* *(Genesis 42:22).*

I think it's safe to say that we have stood where Joseph stood at some point in life. Knowing Christ has forgiven us of our sins, and He has given us a chance at eternal life, yet we pale when it comes to reciprocating the same forgiveness to our offenders; this is a *test*. We minimize His forgiveness and maximize others' offenses; humanity has the most challenging time letting go and *unplugging* when it's been hurt. *Unplugging* is the freedom of God's Mercy that you and I can live in. God *unplugged* our past when He washed away our sins in the watery grave of baptism. Howbeit, even though you see repentance, you want to make sure, by testing, provoking, and somewhat getting even, to know if it's real or not.

There before Joseph's eyes were the ten men that sold him as a slave. They are eating in his dining room…enjoying his fineries…and basking in the delicatessen's he's prepared for them. Unbeknownst to them, Joseph is plotting a plan. Joseph wants to see once and for all if they have genuinely repented for what they did to him.

THE FINAL EXAM

After dinner was finished, and the brothers return to their tents for the evening, their spirits were somewhat high, considering the oddity of their dinner engagement. The food was fabulous, and it was some of the best wine they had ever had. The campsite is littered with tents and livestock, as far as the eye can see. The voices of the sojourners are beginning to diminish as darkness sets in across the land. The glow of campfires lit the evening skies. In the morning, the sons of Israel will start their return to Canaan, with more provision to sustain them during the famine and Simeon and, more importantly, Benjamin.

Meanwhile, Joseph is putting the next phase of his plan into action as he commands his servants.

> *"Fill the men's sacks with food, as much as they can carry,*
> *and put every man's money in his sack's mouth. And put*
> *my cup, the silver cup, in the sack's mouth of the youngest,*

and his corn money." And he did according to the word that Joseph had spoken.

— Genesis 44:1-2

In just a matter of hours, he would see if they had truly changed or were they still the same lying, deceiving, and hateful brothers who sold him out over twenty years ago! Will they be so willing to sell Benjamin out, like they did him? Will they even return to Egypt and try to redeem him, or will they devise some lie between themselves to tell their father if Benjamin is taken?

As soon as the morning was light, the men were sent away, they and their asses.

— Genesis 44:3

As the distant drone of Egypt's noise diminished, they were finally headed home, where Jacob would be impatiently anticipating their return. An overwhelming weight had been lifted off their shoulders, not only because Simeon was freed from imprisonment but also because Benjamin was safe and sound, and their lie was still concealed.

And when they were gone out of the city, and not yet far off, Joseph said unto his steward, "Up, follow after the men; and when thou dost overtake them, say unto them, Wherefore have ye rewarded evil for good"? "Is not this it in which my lord drinketh, and whereby indeed he divineth? ye have done evil in so doing."

— Genesis 44:4-5

Bantering back and forth to shake off the nerves and the stress from what they had just experienced, in an attempt to put behind them this whole ordeal --relieved to be headed home. It wouldn't be long before the brothers rejoined their families, and life would return to normal. Excitement teemed in their spirits at the thought of seeing everyone. However, a faint noise caught their attention, lowering their voices to distinguish what it was? It was the sound of galloping hooves drawing nearer unto them. Turning to see who and what was approaching them, instantly, their laughter turned to silence. Every man's countenance fell at what they saw. It was the furious riding of the guard's captain for the Lord of Egypt. A nervous gut feeling enveloped them. It's that sixth sense that kicks in and tells you, *"this is not good, and something bad is about to happen."* As the men approached, it was apparent their message came with haste.

> *And he overtook them, and he spake unto them these same words:*
>
> *"Wherefore saith my lord these words?... "Wherefore have ye rewarded evil for good"..." Is not this it in which my lord drinketh, and whereby indeed he divineth"?..." Ye have done evil in so doing."*
>
> *– Genesis 44:6,4-5*

In their panic-stricken state of confusion, dismounting their beasts to prove their innocence to their accuser, they make an outlandish statement:

> *"Behold, the money, which we found in our sacks' mouths, we brought again unto thee out of the land of Canaan: how then should we steal out of thy lord's house silver or gold?"*
>
> *"With whomsoever of thy servants it be found, both let him die, and we also will be my lord's bondmen." And he said, "Now also let it be according unto your words: he with whom it is found shall be my servant; and ye shall be blameless."*
>
> *– Genesis 44:6-10*

How many times in your life have you said something you wished you never had? As the words are leaving your mouth and audibly enter into your ears, you say to yourself, *"why did I just say that?"* At that very moment, you regret your words. There's no turning back; the damage is done. You can't pull them out of the air, and they have just fallen on the ears of whom they were intended for. Now the train of consequence follows, and you brace yourself for the impact. I've heard an old saying in my life, over the last twenty-plus years, of serving the Lord, and I feel it very applicable to what the brothers of Joseph have just done, and it says, *"You've been hung by the tongue."* Their rebuttal to the accuser's accusation was the coup de grace.

> *Then they speedily took down every man his sack to the ground, and opened every man his sack. And he searched, and began at the eldest, and left at the youngest: and the cup was found in Benjamin's sack. Then they rent their clothes.*
> — *Genesis 44:11-13*

The milieu was intense. *"OH MY GOD,"* raced through every brother's mind as it would yours as the captain of the guard pulled the silver cup from Benjamin's sack. With a menacing glare, the captain of the guard turned and stared at them. One by one, they began to speak, interrupt, and talk over one another in a desperate attempt to explain the unexplainable. Indeed, there was a mistake; that couldn't be the Lord of Egypt's cup; they never even came close to his table; shepherds are an abomination. How could this thing be? This thought just occurred to me, and this is purely speculation. But just maybe, and I mean maybe, Joseph wanted his brothers to feel what it was like to be lied on. Maybe Joseph wanted them to feel what it was like when Potiphar's wife accused him of attempted rape, and he was defenseless, his word against her word, a

THOMAS L. TEAL JR

losing battle? The helpless feeling of being framed for a crime you didn't commit. Welcome to Joseph's world!

Not only have they sealed their fate, but they have also sealed Benjamin's too. No words can describe the confused and agonizing state of their chafed minds as they watched the silver cup of Joseph's being extracted out of Benjamin's sack. Held high in the air for all to see was the Lord of Egypt's silver cup, shimmering in the sunlight as the sun's rays reflecting off it, signifying guilty as charged. In great horror and disbelief, "*They rent their clothes,*" the token of sorrow that knows no remedy. Benjamin was now destined to be a slave like Joseph, whom they sold. How would they explain this to their father? They tried to reason with the guard, but it was to no avail. They headed back to Egypt; the trek was excruciating. Everyone's mind was racing, including Benjamins, who realized his fate; he would be a slave to the Lord of Egypt.

> *Judah and his brethren came to Joseph's house; for he was yet there: and they fell before him on the ground. Joseph said unto them, "What deed is this that ye have done? wot ye not that such a man as I can certainly divine?"*
> — Genesis 44:14-15

Lucid in his address, Joseph accosted his brothers with a tongue-lashing. The harvest had *come full circle.* There they stood helpless, like Joseph, the day he watched them exchange money for his soul. The tables have turned, and now they were on the auction block.

Framed for a crime they didn't commit, they would now feel what he felt, as he was tried and convicted for a crime he didn't commit. Joseph would impose the judgment as of the supreme authority over their life, like they did over his, when he pleaded for them, not to sell him...over twenty years of pent-up hurts and anger... over twenty years of waiting for this day.... Joseph would now seize his moment of reprisal.

And Judah said, "What shall we say unto my lord? what shall we speak? or how shall we clear ourselves"? "God hath found out the iniquity of thy servants: behold, we are my lord's servants, both we, and he also with whom the cup is found."

— Genesis 44:16

"Really, Judah?" It would have been my first thought, and possibly it may have been Joseph's too? Of all people, Judah, who do you think you are? Judah, the natural-born leader of the family...Judah, who it was said, the scepter would never depart from.....Judah, you were the one who brainstormed the idea to sell Joseph off .....Judah's words haunted Joseph for over twenty years. *"What profit is it if we slay our brother and conceal his blood? Come, and let us sell him to the Ishmeelites, and let not our hand be upon him" (Genesis 37:26).* Judah, now you want to play the spokesman for the brothers, with some half-hearted plea of desperation.

However, as Joseph drew neared unto his older brother, something was different. It wasn't the same Judah as it was twenty-two years ago, standing there before him; no, this man was crestfallen. His face bore the markings of his age. Recessed in his forehead and in his cheeks were the wrinkles of time. Crow's feet rested at the corners of his eyes from the years of squinting, trying to block out the desert's sun. His skin toughened like leather from the constant exposure to the elements while tending sheep. Judah was an older man, a man whose personal life had seen its fair share of tragedy. Two of Judah's sons had been killed because of their wickedness against the Lord. The wages of sin had reaped their harvest in his life. Judah's failures as a brother, a father, and a son had changed him. Although Joseph didn't know these things, he could tell life had changed the man standing humbly before him, who was once so willing to sell him out.

They were in no position to do anything contrary or make any sudden attempts to escape; they were surrounded by Joseph's guards. Joseph was still unsure of their sincerity, and his own feelings decided to give them one more final test, to see if Judah and his brethren were sincere in their change. Were they genuinely sorry for what they had done to him, or was this some pseudo repentance and they were simply telling him what he wanted to hear?

> *Joseph says, "God forbid that I should do so: but the man*
> *in whose hand the cup is found, he shall be my servant; and*
> *as for you, get you up in peace unto your father."*
> *— Genesis 44:17*

It was as if time stood still as Joseph's words ricocheted off the walls and returned to pierce their hearts. Jacob's face flashed before their eyes, as his last words to them came screaming in their ears, *"All These Things Are Against Me,"* and *"If I be bereaved of my children, I am bereaved."* The sickle had found its home, and the reaper had begun to harvest the fruit of his crop. Joseph's words were their worst fear. The inconceivable had just become their reality. Benjamin was to be enslaved, and they were told to return back to their father. The thought of returning without Benjamin was more than they could bear. Without Benjamin, facing Jacob would surely be the death of the old man, and every brother knew it; the moment of truth had arrived!

TRUE REPENTANCE IS THE TIPPING POINT

Even though he wasn't the firstborn, Judah's inherent trait marked him as a natural-born leader. His pedigree is marred by mistakes and woes. Usually, however, every great leader has had significant failures in their life, and Judah was no exception. Instead of taking the high road and evading the consequences, he follows through with his promise to

Jacob. This time it would be different, unlike twenty-two years ago, when he looked into his father's eyes and told him that Joseph was killed by a wild beast of the field.

They all could have turned their backs on Benjamin and walked away. After all, it was the command from the Lord of Egypt. Something welled up in Judah that no one had ever seen before. Life, and the trials and afflictions that come with it, build a particular character that otherwise goes undeveloped. Judah, the aged man, was now willing to find the courage and take responsibility as a leader. Judah could have fabricated another lie to save himself instead of falling on the sword. No, not this time; this time, it was going to be different.

> Then Judah came near unto him, and said, "Oh my lord, let thy servant, I pray thee, speak a word in my lord's ears, and let not thine anger burn against thy servant: for thou art even as Pharaoh." "My lord asked his servants, saying, Have ye a father, or a brother?" "And we said unto my lord, We have a father, an old man, and a child of his old age, a little one; and his brother is dead, and he alone is left of his mother, and his father loveth him." "And thou saidst unto thy servants, Bring him down unto me, that I may set mine eyes upon him."
>
> "And we said unto my lord, The lad cannot leave his father: for if he should leave his father, his father would die. "And thou saidst unto thy servants, Except your youngest brother come down with you, ye shall see my face no more."
> – Genesis 44:18-23

Like a defense attorney representing a guilty party, Judah begins his litigation. Judah started pleading his case before the grand jury; his voice-inflections are an exhibition of woefulness as he articulates his defense. His appeal to sway a looming verdict is evident as he continues in his delivery.

> *"And our father said, Go again, and buy us a little food."* *"And we said, We cannot go down: if our youngest brother be with us, then will we go down: for we may not see the man's face, except our youngest brother be with us." "And thy servant my father said unto us, Ye know that my wife bare me two sons." "And the one went out from me, and I said, Surely he is torn in pieces; and I saw him not since." "And if ye take this also from me, and mischief befall him, ye shall bring down my gray hairs with sorrow to the grave."*
>
> *– Genesis 44:25-29*

A slight pause in his delivery allowed his words to sink in and have their full effect, from his desperate cry. Not only had his voice revealed the admission of guilt, but it had also now taken on the distinct sound of contrition and regret; in Judah's words were mingled the undertones of grief. Unwilling to bear his father's death, Judah continues with his appeal in hopes of thwarting the Lord of Egypt's judgment.

> *"Now therefore when I come to thy servant my father, and the lad be not with us; seeing that his life is bound up in the lad's life." "It shall come to pass, when he seeth that the lad is not with us, that he will die: and thy servants shall bring down the gray hairs of thy servant our father with sorrow to the grave." "For thy servant became surety for the lad unto my father, saying, If I bring him not unto thee, then I shall bear the blame to my father forever." "Now therefore, I pray thee, let thy servant abide instead of the lad a bondman to my lord; and let the lad go up with his brethren." "For*

how shall I go up to my father, and the lad be not with me?
lest peradventure I see the evil that shall come on my father."
— *Genesis 44:30-34*

The silence was deafening after Judah closed with his final statement to the court. Hoping his surety profession would be the tipping point to sway the looming judgment, he waits for a response. Not only was Judah sorry, so were his brothers. The years of concealing their crime had tortured their souls. Their countenance told a story of humiliation and remorse for what they had done to him.

There they stood, the perpetrators of his pain, broken and dejected for their sin was the crushing blow to Joseph's heart. Joseph is trembling inside at what he had just witnessed--the walls begin to crumble. At last, Joseph saw his brother's true repentance. The Lord of Egypt utters a stern command in Egyptian, feeling naked and vulnerable, unwilling to reveal and unveil his true identity. In an instant, all of his servants depart from the room at once. The dining hall is void of everyone, save that of the Lord of Egypt and Jacob's eleven sons. Unsure of why all the servants have just left the room so abruptly --trepidation seep into their souls. There they stood alone for the first time in twenty-two years together in the same place; together, once again, like the dreadful day, when they sold Joseph as a slave. There is a deafening silence in the room, now visibly shaken; the lump in his throat begins to swell. Like a volcano ready to erupt and release all of its internal pressure, Joseph cannot hold back the pain. The tears burst forth and erupt, streaming down his cheeks like molten lava; Joseph bow's his head into his hands as he is overtaken with emotion. Twenty-two years of bottled-up pain inside of him burst like a broken dam.

THE HEALING BALM OF FORGIVENESS IS THE HEALING OF YOUR OWN WOUNDS

And he wept aloud: and the Egyptians and the house of Pharaoh heard. And Joseph said unto his brethren, "I am Joseph; doth my father yet live?" And his brethren could not answer him; for they were troubled at his presence.

And Joseph said unto his brethren, "Come near to me, I pray you. And they came near. And he said, I am Joseph your brother, whom ye sold into Egypt." "Now therefore be not grieved, nor angry with yourselves, that ye sold me hither: for God did send me before you to preserve life." "For these two years hath the famine been in the land: and yet there are five years, in the which there shall neither be earing nor harvest." "And God sent me before you to preserve you a posterity in the earth, and to save your lives by a great deliverance."

– Genesis 45:2-7

The conundrum of God's Will in your life and its wondrous workings can be seen in the life of Joseph. There will be times in your life, like Joseph, when you can't help but wonder if God is even around. Utter depravity surrounds you, and your life seems destitute of what God promised in His Word. Like Joseph, and his father Jacob, you will wrestle with the thought of wondering why *"All these things are against me;" "You've come full circle."* Will you let go of the pain? Will you turn it over to God, like Joseph did? For his brother's wickedness towards him, Joseph's forgiveness was not only his healing but also his brother's healing. If Joseph had refused to let go and trust God, we wouldn't have one of the greatest stories of forgiveness in the Bible. There are so many lessons to be taken away from the story of Joseph. What started out as an extreme act of jealousy and hatred became one of a Christian life's most incredible examples.

God is so multi-dimensional in every facet of His Will, working in ways beyond our understanding. He used anger, jealousy, and betrayal to set up a great deliverance beyond human reasoning and comprehension! Allowing innocence to be robbed from a young man…allowing him to be set up and falsely accused…wrongfully imprisoned…leaving him to feel helpless and impoverished in a prison cell.

It's hard to find the sovereignty of God in this. I don't believe Joseph ever imagined that he would one day become second in command to Pharaoh and a prince in Egypt while in prison. When Joseph interpreted Pharaoh's dreams, he never envisioned those dreams would one day re-unite him with his brothers, let alone his father. Things are not always what they appear to be --God had to allow Joseph to go through what he did to become what God needed him to be, a deliverer!

The mystery of the "why's" and "what's" of God's Will is sometimes not revealed until further down the road. Don't judge your present situation because it seems hopeless now. You may have come *"full circle,"* but it's only set up for something extraordinary in your life. In the emptiness of our own prison cell, we can't see what's beyond the four walls that surround us. Sometimes you have to become a prisoner, to be a deliverer. To become a deliverer, you first have to become a forgiver. In order to become a forgiver, you have to realize that you have been forgiven. You have to *unplug* and stop living in the pains of the past, caused by others. Instead, reach out to help others, like Christ helped you.

CHAPTER 10

TO LIVE IS TO DIE THE GREAT PARADOX OF "UNPLUGGING" FROM SELF

"He must increase, but I must decrease."

– John 3:30

We live in the day and age where egotism and self-conceit riddle the media. Tabloids and tweets of the social elites in Hollywood are plastered across the internet. It seems the more the rich have, the more is given unto them—nothing against wealth. I'm a firm believer in hard work should pay very well. However, wealth should never replace God. God hasn't blessed your life with the intention of possessions being your focal point and not Him.

Today, most people find it easier to give to those who have, instead of giving to those who don't. By doing so, they somehow feel equal to the affluent. No, I'm not saying everybody who has financial freedom is selfish or has never given those who have not. Howbeit, I have read and witnessed aristocratic favoritism. Too often, the monetary value of things is equated to giving. This couldn't be further from the truth. Nothing is more valuable than life, and the more you give of it, the greater the blessing becomes. Things can be replaced by life, but life can't be replaced by things.

Today, the medical and psychological terminology validates the self-sickness that has not only crept in but practically taken over. Terms labeling human behavior and exposing the way man's nature is driven. Idioms like Narcissism…*Egotism…Self-Centeredness…Entitlement;* are reliable indicators of where we are and what we've become. Procured by the notion that *"I"* come before *"we"* have been why this country has digressed as a once known Christian nation. However, there is no *medical terminology* given to those who prefer others before themselves. Why is this? Because this is *"The great paradox of unplugging from self!"*

The Apostle Paul, in his letter to the young pastor, Timothy, would describe in detail the condition of man in the last days. Paul writes, *"This know also, that in the last days perilous times shall come. For men shall be lovers of their own selves, covetous, boasters, proud, blasphemers, disobedient to parents, unthankful, unholy, Without natural affection, trucebreakers, false accusers, incontinent, fierce, despisers of those that are good."* (2Tim 3:1-3) Everyone is guilty in some form or another, of living in the *"I"* mode. The difference between the world, and yourself, is your ability, through the Word of God, to recognize it and change it.

John the Baptist, the forerunner of Jesus Christ, made such a selfless statement, *"He must increase, but I must decrease."* This was a paradigm shift in the philosophy of his day's religious leaders and those of today. John knew his time on earth would be short-lived and that the whole purpose of his life was to promote and prepare the way for Christ. John's ministry was the catalyst of what would become the ushering-in of a New Covenant. Clothed in camel skin and a leather girdle about his loins, a diet of locust and honey would be his epitaph. A messenger groomed in the wilderness and a preacher on riverbanks would be his legacy. John's message addressed the heart; he preached baptism, repentance, and confession of sin. John preached against the self-righteous and pompous spirits of his day. Unlike anything of his time, John's delivery was scathing rebukes, laced with metaphors and similes, in his verbal manifesto's; articulating terminology, revealing a navel-gazing, and conceited *"generation of vipers,"* as he so eloquently put it.

Like John, your calling is to promote Christ and not yourself. Not only was this John's statement about his ministry, but his life. John knew as he decreased, Christ would increase. Jesus said, *"If I be lifted up from the earth, I will draw all men unto me."* A clear and pronounced statement indicating who and what will be exalted and what intent and purpose it was for. The purpose, you ask? Yes, the purpose is to draw souls unto Christ through self-denial. To decrease is to let go and lift up God. *"Self"* wants to live and not die and has a hard time letting go. *"Self"* wants what it wants, when it wants, what it wants. The Lord Jesus never lived in the *"I"* mode. *I came down from heaven, **NOT** to do mine own Will, but the Will of Him that sent me (John 6:38).* Christ lived, *"The Great Paradox!*

If *we* genuinely want to be like Christ, then *we* must die to self-desire. The Lord Jesus Christ came into this world with one resolve to bring salvation to man. Man, had become complacent in his walk with God, being justified with the external commandment of sacrifices and ordinances--but never addressing matters of the heart. Under the law, a man was not guilty of his wicked thoughts or evil intentions, as long as he didn't break one of the commandments, i.e., *eating unclean animals, touching a dead body, or doing servile work on the Sabbath,* he was righteous before God. When Christ came into this world, He exposed the wickedness of man's heart and the Law's faultiness. Moses law taught, *"An eye for an eye, a tooth for a tooth,"* but Christ taught, *"Whosoever shall smite thee on thy right cheek, turn to him the other also."* The sermon on the Mountain in Matthew's Gospel is a rendering of *"The Perfect Law Of Liberty."* Christ accentuates the Spiritual aspect of what the Law intended but could never accomplish in His sermon. Epiphanies like, *"Blessed are the pure in heart for they shall see God...Blessed are they that hunger and thirst for righteousness...Blessed* *are the merciful for they shall obtain mercy…Blessed are they that which are persecuted for righteousness…*were the antidotes for the Spiritual blindness in the Old Testament Law.

> *"If any man will come after me, let him deny himself, and take up his cross daily, and follow me."*
>
> *– Matthew 16:24*

Christ reveals where the real battle lies and what John meant when he said, *"He must increase, but I must decrease."* This is what a Christian must endeavor to do every day of their life; take up their cross and deny *"I,"* the paradox of unplugging. If anybody could have had a justified attitude, it was Jesus. All He did was reach out to help others; in return, He got mostly hostility; and sadly enough, it came from the very ones He was trying to help. *"He came unto His own, and His own received Him not"* *(John 1:11).* They kicked Him out of their synagogue. They attempted to throw Him off a cliff. They accused Him of blasphemy, yet at His death, He makes the most selfless statement ever, *"Father, forgive them; for they know not what they do!"* What did they do? They killed Christ because of His self-denial message, coupled with His rebuke towards their indignant self-righteous attitudes. Christ exposed the Law's failure when He revealed that one must first clean the cup inside before cleaning the outside. This infuriated them to the point of murder when He likened them unto, *"Whited sepulchers, which indeed appear beautiful outward, but are within full of dead men's bones."* Furious at His words furthered His message. The great paradox of being unplugged. It starts on the inside and then moves to the outside.

IT'S NOT ABOUT YOU; IT'S ABOUT UNPLUGGING FROM SELF

"The Secret Of Living Is Giving"

– Pastor W.J. Davidson

This is probably one of the hardest things to do; *unplug from self* and give to others. It's easier for most to give someone money for a need, give one's personal time, and sacrifice things you want to do for someone else's betterment requires a cross of self-denial. The statement above is from my Pastor; it summarizes a message that many overlook because they're consumed by self-indulgence.

The Lord Jesus Christ was the essence of selflessness and the pinnacle of giving! The Lord never looked down on those of misfortune…He never denied others to prefer Himself…He never wanted accolades when He would perform a miracle; His mantra was, *"Tell no man."* Jesus simply lived the *"secret of giving,"* and without fail, he always came to the needs of others. Take a look at the list below at this selfless God.

- Converts Water To Wine At A Wedding When They Ran Out – John 2:1-11
- Heals The Paralyzed Man – Matthew 9:1-8
- Restoring The Withered Hand – Mark 3:1-5
- Stops A Procession In Nain, And Raises A Widows Son – Luke 7:11-16
- Cures The Woman With An Issue Of Blood – Mark 5:25-34
- Heals The Epileptic Boy – Matthew 17:14-21
- Feeds More Than Four Thousand People – Mark 8:19
- Restores Sight To A Blind Man – Mark 8:22-26
- Cleanses The Lepers Of Their Leprosy – Luke 17:11-19

*The word **"Christian"** means: Treating other people in a kind and generous way as Christ did!*

To be a Christian is to be like Christ. Not only in your speech but in your thoughts and in your actions towards others. The only time the Lord Jesus Christ was *"offensive"* in His actions and speech towards others is when the Scribes and Pharisees would try to twist Moses's law and use it against Him. People will try to find your faults simply because you have them. They'll discredit any good you are trying to accomplish because of your imperfections. They will justify their faults because of yours. No matter what they say or what they do, you still have to love them because it's not about you. It's about Him--because in most cases, they simply *"know not what they do."*

> *"And the lord said unto the servant, Go out into the highways and hedges, and compel them to come in, that my house may be filled."*
>
> *— Luke 14:23*

Whether you know this or not? Part of the "Great paradox of *unplugging"* is reaching out to others. I know that not everybody feels comfortable talking to random strangers and striking up a conversation with them. My wife Laura, on the other hand, is that person. Laura has fantastic people skills. We'll be waiting in line for dinner or at some store, even at the airport. She'll strike up a conversation with the person standing next to us like she's known them her entire life--It's a gift from God. I'm a salesman by trade, and when I'm on a sales call, I have an objective; making the sale. They've called our company because they have a need, and we have their solution, and it's my job to ensure it. In the early years of our business, the internet wasn't available, and our only means of advertising was door-to-door sales, otherwise known as cold-calling. Jesus commanded the disciples to compel, or door-to-door, cold-call people to come to His feast.

I am a firm proponent of outreach programs, and I have personally been involved with them where we have gone door-to-door, cold-calling people to the Lord's House. I would like to share with you an experience we encountered in our endeavors to compel the lost. Our outreach program went out door to door on a warm summer day, inviting local residents in our neighborhood to church. We prayed before we set out and asked the Lord to direct our steps, and He did. Unbeknownst to us, there was a little old lady in her 80's that had the heart to know the truth and had been seeking God; her name was Ruth.

She had a withered hand, crippled over and walked with a cane, but had a hunger for the Lord. We knocked on her door on that bright sunny Saturday afternoon, Ruth opened it up to us, and we shared the Gospel with her. Ruth asked us to pray for her, and we gladly obliged. Before we left, we invited her to church. Ruth said she would love to come but couldn't drive. One of the gentlemen said he and his wife would pick her up. A marvelous miracle transpired in Ruth's life when she came to church that Sunday. God filled her with the Holy Ghost, and she was baptized in Jesus' name, fell in love with the truth, and never missed a Sunday service after that. A few months had passed, and the couple went to pick Ruth up on Sunday, and they were informed by Ruth's neighbors, she had passed during the week. Had it not been for someone taking a Saturday out of their busy schedule to do something for the Lord and not themselves, Ruth may have never heard the gospel of her salvation.

Could I or the gentlemen that were with me could have worked on that Saturday and made money for our families? Yes. However, you cannot put a monetary value on what happened that Saturday morning when Ruth heard the gospel of her salvation and wanted to come to church. To live is to die. The paradox of unplugging from self was manifest that Sunday morning when Ruth came to church and was filled with the Spirit of God.

Maybe you don't feel comfortable in large crowds or talking to strangers? That's okay because sometimes the best sermons ever heard are the ones seen lived. Let your life preach a message to this world that's your witness. Let your actions and manner of life become your unspoken words. I've had customers ask me, *"do you go to church"*; when I have never said a word to them about the church. Sometimes just your demeanor of living in obedience to God's Word will be the very catalyst that opens up the door of opportunity. Jesus said, *"And I if I be lifted up from the earth, I will draw all men unto me" (John 12:32)*. Jesus is not only referring to the natural Cross He would hang on, but He's also referring to His life being lived out of yours. It's not a *"Holier Than Thou"* attitude. It's a life lived through obedience that will draw people to Him.

YOUR TESTIMONY IS YOUR GREATEST WITNESS

"No man, when he hath lighted a candle, covereth it with a vessel, or putteth it under a bed; but setteth it on a candlestick, that they which enter in may see the light."
— *Luke 8:16*

Whether you were born in church or came from the world to church, everybody has a testimony. You don't have to come from a background of drugs, alcohol, violence, or abuse to have God give you deliverance and birth a testimony in your life. Sadly, however, such horrible backgrounds seem to be the majority, not the minority these days.

I grew up in a divorced home, we moved from town to town, I went from school to school, and God was not a part of our life. My parents partied when I was younger; they were from the hippie generation, nothing too excessive or out of control to speak of. They had their own personal issues they were dealing with, and drugs and alcohol were their medications. As a teenager, and up until my early twenties, I followed suit, using drugs and alcohol as my medication to anesthetize pain. This seems to be the common thread sewn in the fabric of life for most people coming from the world to Christ. However, the inner workings are entirely different—no one's pain is the same.

The day finally came in January 1993 when I wanted a change. I wanted the misery to end; I was tired of the emptiness of drugs and alcohol and living at rock bottom. After being invited several times to church,

I agreed to go; what did I have to lose? My life was an upside-down mess; my band had fallen apart, and I had recently gotten fired from my job. I wanted to unplug from the chaos that enveloped my life. I was ready to relinquish my will for His Will. It was time for a change, and it couldn't have come at a better time in my life—it was the most significant decision I ever made.

It's hard to believe it's been over twenty-seven years, and now here I am writing a book and sharing with you my testimony about the greatness of God and how your testimony is a Light for the World to see Jesus.

"Actions Speak Louder Than Words" is a phrase often heard throughout life. Your actions are your words, and your words are backed up by faith in God's Word; that's the power of your testimony. When sickness strikes, you speak faith to your illness…when life handed you a bowl of lemons, you made lemonade….when you didn't have money for that bill, you said God was your Jehovah-Jireh, the great provider. Those actions, and your proclamation of faith in God, will one day become the hope and strength for those who are watching you from afar during your darkest hour.

I don't know where and I don't know how, but what I do know from personal experience is God will use what you've gone through, to minister faith in Him, for them. Your pain is not your own…your struggle is not your own…your hurt is not your own…it's all for the Glory of God to shine out of your life…and into the darkness of someone else's self-despair. The Apostle Paul admonishes us that there is a bigger picture than what meets the eye. The things you're going through are not just to make you stronger and closer in your relationship with the Lord; they are to be a comfort and strength for others to draw from.

> *"Blessed be God, even the Father of our Lord Jesus*
> *Christ, the Father of mercies, and the God of all comfort;"*
> *"Who comforteth us in all our tribulation, that we may be*

able to comfort them which are in any trouble, by the comfort
wherewith we ourselves are comforted of God."

— 2 Corinthians 1:3-4

Life has a way of teaching us lessons a book or a teacher never could, and some lessons are not fully understood until years down the road. At times, and in those moments, of what appears to be a whirlwind of doom, the thought of something good ever coming out is so far removed. Overwhelmed and distraught, it's inconceivable to envision a testimony amid the fray. It feels like your soul has been eviscerated from the pain. In his writing to the Corinthian church, Paul shares his testimony with the church to inspire saints struggling with trials and persecutions—he writes.

"I am in stripes above measure, in prisons more frequent,
in deaths oft. Of the Jews five times received I forty stripes
save one." "Thrice was I beaten with rods, once was I stoned,
thrice I suffered shipwreck, a night and a day I have been in
the deep." "In journeyings often, in perils of waters, in perils
of robbers, in perils by mine own countrymen, in perils by
the heathen, in perils in the city, in perils in the wilderness,
in perils in the sea, in perils among false brethren."
"In weariness and painfulness, in watchings often, in
hunger and thirst, in fastings often, in cold and nakedness."
"Beside those things that are without, that which cometh
upon me daily, the care of all the churches." "Who is weak,
and I am not weak? who is offended, and I burn not?" "If
I must needs glory, I will glory of the things which concern
mine infirmities." "The God and Father of our Lord Jesus
Christ, which is blessed for evermore, knoweth that I lie not".
"In Damascus the governor under Aretas the king kept the

city of the Damascenes with a garrison, desirous to apprehend me." "And through a window in a basket was I let down by the wall, and escaped his hands."

– 2 Corinthians 11:23-33

I have yet to meet anybody who has endured such trials and hardships for preaching the Word of God. These verses of scripture are humbling and inspiring at the same time. Paul epitomizes what it is to suffer for the inspiration of others. We live sheltered lives and can't even relate to what it's like to live under such strenuous conditions as Paul did in his ministry in America. Yet, he says it's for the glory and comfort of others. The Bible is the Living Word of inspiration. It's a book showing and revealing the Word of God, lived out of saints' lives, who put faith above their circumstances.

Job is a prime example; his life was struck with a calamity and shattered into endless pieces —a book comprised of a man suffering for the sake of others' salvation. If you ever think you're having a bad day, just read the first few chapters of his autobiography, and you'll soon realize it could be worse.

And there came a messenger unto Job, and said, "The oxen were plowing, and the asses feeding beside them." "And the Sabeans fell upon them, and took them away; yea, they have slain the servants with the edge of the sword; and I only am escaped alone to tell thee." While he was yet speaking, there came also another, and said, " The fire of God is fallen from heaven, and hath burned up the sheep, and the servants, and consumed them; and I only am escaped alone to tell thee."

While he was yet speaking, there came also another, and said, "The Chaldeans made out three bands, and fell upon

the camels, and have carried them away, yea, and slain the
servants with the edge of the sword; and I only am escaped
alone to tell thee." While he was yet speaking, there came also
another, and said, 'Thy sons and thy daughters were eating
and drinking wine in their eldest brother's house: And, be-
hold, there came a great wind from the wilderness, and smote
the four corners of the house, and it fell upon the young men,
and they are dead; and I only am escaped alone to tell thee".

— Job 1:14-19

Job's children were taken from him in one day, his livestock was taken from him...his wealth was taken from him...his health was taken from him, smitten with boils from head to toe! In one day, everything was gone! I can't even imagine the pain this man endured in those horrifying moments. Wave after wave of death and destruction came ashore in Job's life that day. It was devastation unheralded. I have lost a child, and it's devastating, but to lose everything in one fell-swoop--incomprehensible!

Then Job arose, and rent his mantle, and shaved his
head, and fell down upon the ground, and worshipped, And
said, "Naked came I out of my mother's womb, and naked
shall I return thither: the LORD gave, and the LORD hath
taken away; blessed be the name of the LORD." In all this
Job sinned not, nor charged God foolishly.

— Job 1:20-22

I want you to pause right now and reread *Job 1:14-19*. Place yourself in this man's shoes. Imagine sitting in the comforts of your home, you're wealthy, and you don't have a need or want. All the fineries that life can afford you, God has so abundantly blessed you with. Let that sink in because that's where Job was at.

Job was the richest man in the east, esteemed a dignitary, and men stood in the marketplace when he passed by. Like Job, you're living for God with everything in you. You fast every week, you have a devoted prayer life, and you read the Word of God without fail. You never miss a church service; you give your tithes and offerings faithfully and support every work in the church. Indeed, one wouldn't imagine being a witness and the salvation of another person's soul; would require going through such horrific extremes? Wouldn't a blessed life be enough to inspire someone to live for God and embrace all His goodness?

Apparently, this wasn't the case with Job, and maybe this is the same with you? Not only was Job's trial for the salvation of the men he dubbed *"Miserable Comforters, Forgers of lies and Physicians of No Value,"* this trial was for Job and his salvation too.

Jealousy and contempt were filled in their hearts towards Job. They railed, belittled, and were fault-finding for forty chapters, criticizing Job's life and his walk with God. Accusation after accusation, they accused him of hypocritical ways, disparaging and rebuffed any notion of Job's virtue. Taunts and tongue-lashings in an attempt to prevail against a crumpled man, a man whose life had been shattered in a moment.

You read about it, and it's hard to wrap your head around it, but for some people, they find pleasure in watching people suffer. This sickness stems from insecurities and personal abuse they have suffered somewhere in their lives; they were victims of some sort. Abuse has many forms and fashions, verbally or physically. It's like the little boy who grew up watching his dad beat his mother. As a little boy, he hated hearing and seeing his mother cry from his father's abuse, yet he finds himself repeating the same violent behavior towards his wife when he grows up. The adult, who was abused as a child, is now abusing their child. The child, who grew up with an alcoholic parent, soon finds themselves becoming an alcoholic, and the cycle continues on.

However, many people have risen from the depths of despair and made something for themselves and their families. Such a one is David Goggins. Goggins is a retired Navy Seal, and he has written a book entitled, "You can't hurt me." In it, he shares his life story and the many struggles he's had to overcome, and what it took for him to become a Navy Seal--one of the most respected positions in our military. David talks a lot about mind over matter, and that's really the battlefield we have to fight on. Now is the time to rise above those negative thoughts that want to keep you down and out. You're standing on the battlefield (your mind), and you're waging war on the enemy within. It's time to *unplug* from self-condemnation and self-deprivation, and whatever it is that keeps telling you you're not good enough; because you are. *For if our heart condemn us, God is greater than our heart, and knoweth all things (1 John 3:20).* God knows... God sees everything you've gone through, and like Job, His greatness is going to shine out of your life, and your testimony is going to be one-day somebody's salvation.

Job's life was laid waste as he stood at the gravesites of his deceased children. Job could have gotten mad at God and thrown the towel in like I've seen people do in similar situations. They say, *"this just isn't worth it anymore."* Job's calamity exposed the dark matters of his accuser's heart towards him, Job's three friends (Eliphaz, Bildad, Zophar). They railed on Job, chapter after chapter picking him apart and finding every fault he had, proclaiming they were the reason his life was full of calamity. *"To Live Is To Die."*

Job would not only have to forgive them, but he would also have to pray God's mercy in their life. Unbeknownst to Job, not only would his prayer thwart God's wrath in his friend's lives, but it would also turn his captivity and yield a blessing beyond his imagination.

In Job story, you gain the strength, faith, and confidence that God will see you through in your darkest hours! When my wife and I lost our daughter at birth, Scarlet Hope Teal, I had people said that this would be our end. They thought we would stop serving the Lord after all our daughter died, and we have given our entire life to him. On a Thursday night, our daughter passed, and on that following Sunday morning Church service, Pastor Davidson, preached a message entitled *"When Bad Things Happen To Good People"*—he drew his text from the book of Job. There is a misconception people adhere to, in which they believe because you're serving the Lord, tragedy won't strike your life. I'm living proof; it can and will happen. This is not to say that every person who gives their life to the Lord should brace themselves for such great woes.

There are seasons in life where the *"Great Paradox of To Live Is To Die"* becomes very real. Real, because the ultimate death is *"self,"* you must kill the inner voices that want to turn their back on God when you're faced with a trial like Job. You have to *unplug* from yourself and *plug* into God; it's a walk of faith, not sight. The definition of "faith" in its most raw organic form is simply complete trust. *"Though he slay me, yet will I trust in him" (Job 13:15).*

JOBS TESTIMONY:

> So the LORD blessed the latter end of Job more than his
> beginning: for he had fourteen thousand sheep, and six thou-
> sand camels, and a thousand yoke of oxen, and a thousand
> she asses. He had also seven sons and three daughters.
> — Job 42:12-13

Job probably could have never imagined thousands of years, after his life had passed, that its impact would be so significant on the many lives it would touch. His life and the trials he endured while trusting the Lord would minister to so many people. Your life is a living epistle this world is reading; the trials and tribulations you go through and endure are touching the lives of those watching. Job never could have believed it, as he sat amongst the heap of ashes that once were his possessions, that his life would be filled with joy again. At that moment, to believe he could be restored was unfathomable. Your present situation doesn't define you, nor does it confine you; it merely refines you, so you can become a deliverer. The best is yet to come; it's not over. At the end of Job's life, you see the faithfulness of God and the richness of the Lord.

> "We know how happy they are now because they stayed true to him then, even though they suffered greatly for it." "Job is an example of a man who continued to trust the Lord in sorrow; from his experiences, we can see how the Lord's plan finally ended in good, for he is full of tenderness and mercy."
>
> — James 5:11-12 TLB

Things will get better, God cannot lie, and it is a promise in His Word; you can count on it. Job and many others who have walked through the fiery trials of this life, trusting God, have shown us the graciousness of the Lord. If Job had got mad, gave up, and walked away from God, he never would have seen the goodness of the Lord come to pass. The Lord gave him double for his trouble, and He'll do the same for you.

> "Fight the good fight of faith, lay hold on eternal life, whereunto thou art also called, and hast professed a good profession before many witnesses."
>
> — 1 Timothy 6:12

Job knew that quitting was not an option. His life professed that God was his God, and so does yours. It's not about this life; it's about eternal life and making sure you make it all the way--it's going to be a fight. Job's choice to "die" so that others could "live" was a great paradox. His prayer saved their lives, and so does yours for your friends and loved ones. You have to trust God in good times and bad because things are not always as they appear. *"To live is to die is a great paradox,"* and the secret of *"unplugging."*

> *"For whosoever will save his life shall lose it: and whoso-*
> *ever will lose his life for my sake shall find it."*
>
> *– Matthew 16:25*

CHAPTER 11

UNPLUGGED AND ACCEPTING THE CHALLENGE!

The word "CHALLENGE" has many meanings, and I have selected the ones that I believe defines the concept of what you are doing:

- to confront or defy boldly
- to call out to duel or combat
- to invite into competitions
- to make or present a challenge

Take a deep breath, inhale, and then exhale; you got this.

- Forty days to defy and boldly come up against the mainstream.
- Forty days to call out and combat the oppositions of the human appetite.
- Forty days to compete against your own will and to conquer its desires.
- Forty days to finish a personal challenge.

If you choose to accept the challenge over the next forty days, you will begin to write your catalog: spiritually and naturally. *"Unplugged"* is not only a challenge; it's a lifestyle. A lifestyle that encompasses victory, freedom, and joy. There are several illustrations in the Bible of 40-day challenges, and I want to show a few of them to you.

TEMPTED IN THE WILDERNESS - TEMPTED IN LIFE

And when he (Christ) had fasted forty days and forty nights, he was afterward an hungerd.

— Matthew 4:2

Matthew 4:1-10 is the beginning of Christ's ministry. I don't believe everything recorded was literal. Yes, turning stones into bread was a real temptation as Christ wrestled with hunger, but sitting on the pinnacle of a temple is impossible. However, jumping off a cliff that could have been probable? But more importantly, I believe it was a battle in the mind of Christ as He prepared to embark on His ministry. The temptations were thoughts that came to Him in His moments of weakness, in the agonizing throes of extreme hunger. Victory against the battle of self-restraint was only possible by 40 days of separation. There will be temptations in your mind and spirit over the next 40 days of this challenge. Just like Christ had to face His temptations, so must you. Growth never comes without discomfort, no pain, no gain. It's in these crippling instants of self-denial is when temptation always comes calling and tells you your labor is futile. The pangs of discomfort will convince you that this is unnecessary, and to be so extreme, to deny oneself for 40 days is stupid. Christ tempted in the wilderness serves as a metaphor, representing man's human nature— it's the enemy of your soul. The human nature of man is corrupt. It lies, steals, cheats, and destroys. Why? Because the inherent nature of man is evil from his birth.

"Man, that is born of a woman is of few days, and full of trouble."

— Job 14:1

Have you ever been in a grocery store and watched a child go into a full-blown tirade, kicking and screaming and lying on the floor, flailing out of control because they couldn't get what they wanted? The parent is looking down at their child, making a spectacle out of themselves. Overwhelmed with embarrassment by the situation and the viewing audience surrounding them. The parent quickly submits to the demands of the child to mitigate the problem. I would venture to say that this is probably not the first time an incident like this has happened, nor will it be the last. The problem is the child does not like to be told "no" because "no" means self-denial. Another assumption I would have to deduct is that there is no real form of discipline in the home either because if there was, the child knows that there would be disciplinary actions taken for such behavior when they got home. So here-in lays your metaphor. When you feel yourself becoming that screaming out-of-control kid you see in the store, who can't have his or her way, let yourself know that if this behavior continues, swift judgment will come in the form of more self-denial.

Like the Lord, who battled the temptation of personal desire in the wilderness, you too will face the same. The Lord spent 40 days on a spiritual mission to conquer a nature He would one day hang on the cross. Truth be told, what Christ killed on the cross was the human nature of man's will. His prayer in Gethsemane encapsulates this, ***"if it be possible, let this cup pass from me, nevertheless not as I will, but as thou wilt."***

THE CROSS

The cup was the cross. The cup was the sacrificing of His human will. Nobody wants to drink from it. The cup looks so much better resting on the shelf than in one's hand to drink from. Over the next forty days, you must drink from the cup and ingest its spiritual substance. Jesus had to conquer His Will before He could teach others to do the same. If you think there is no opposing nature with a will inside you, I challenge you to go forty days without food and only drink water. You will quickly realize how alive the nature inside you is after your first couple of days of fasting.

40 days in the wilderness could not have been avoided. Without the wilderness, there would have never been a resurrection on the third day. Without the 40 days of self-denial, there would have never been a church. Maybe that's the case with some of you? Perhaps, the things you have been allowing to rule in your life are the very things that are stopping you from going forward with what God has in store for your life and possibly a ministry? Now is the time for your wilderness experience. If you are shuttering at the thought of giving something up *(and you know what that is)*, then that's the cup you must drink from. The wilderness is unavoidable if you're going to see the miraculous. Jesus identified the cup and individualized it when he said, **"let him deny himself and take up his cross and follow me."** Your cup isn't my cup, and my cup isn't somebody else's cup. The very word "cross," for some, is detestable.

Either wind-driven or hand-planted, no one knows, the God of all creation was guiding the tender seed into the ground, where it would be planted and take root. His careful eye watched, ensuring its watering and nurturing were met for the sapling, that one day, would bear the weight of his body, for the sins of all humanity. In like fashion, as the vine baring its thorns grew, unknowingly to the vinedresser, it too would one day become the crown that would rest above the brow of an Eternal king. As the egg-formed and the bones grew, and one day life sprang forth from a mother's womb, the announcement of a newborn son echoed in the air. Unbeknownst to her, those cries of joy that filled the air in the room would one day be exchanged for the screams of horror as she watched her firstborn son, lurching and collapsing from the weight of His cross. Reciting Simone's words, on the day of His dedication, *"Yea, a sword shall pierce through thy own soul,"* as they drove the nails into the hands, and feet, of her son, fastening him to a wooden structure. From a seed in the ground to a seed in the womb. The God of all creation watched His crucifiers and crucifix grow, knowing each of them would be the ending point of His life.

The cross identifies in the minds of men as a place of death. The cross symbolizes pain, suffering, and judgment against sin. The cross, stained with the blood and carnage of a sacrifice, offered redemption to mankind. As ugly and horrifying as the cross was, there was no way around it. The thought of your Savior naked, beaten beyond recognition, and hanging there for the world to see makes one wince. Because of His kindness, an innocent man berated and crucified for His people seems convoluted and unfair. The cross is a great paradox. However, as gruesome and grotesque, the cruel sufferings of it would be, it was the sublime will of God. Your cross to bear is nobody else's. At times it might seem unfair and unjust, but it's unavoidable.

There are things in your life you have watched grow from a seed to a sapling, and now into the cross you must bear; throughout the next forty days, you will be in the wilderness on a journey. No, this is not a natural wilderness, though it may seem like it at times; it's a spiritual one. It's a journey of the mind and will; it's a journey unlike any other.

In this journey, you will be tempted by the three major components that entice all humanity; under the Old Testament Law, they were never identified in detail until Christ came and exposed them. During this journey, your spiritual eyesight will be opened in ways you never imagined. Jesus Christ was the ushering-in of the New Testament *(New Will of God)* known as the Perfect Law of Liberty (James 1:25). Christ in the wilderness typified what the New Testament was about to become, and the New Will of God was about to be revealed. In the following scripture, you can see the three failures of mankind that Christ had to conquer in the wilderness, and it gives you an insight into the cross. *"For all that is in the world, the lust of the flesh, and the lust of the eyes, and the pride of life, is not of the Father but is of the world (1 John 2:16).* Christ, had to conquer what makes you ungodly, *the lust of the flesh, the lust of the eyes, and the pride of life,* so you could learn what it is to be Godly.

"Blessed is the man that endureth temptation: for when he is tried, he shall receive the crown of life" (James 1:12). You are going to endure temptations over the next forty days in this wilderness of being *unplugged* to receive your crown. The word *"endure,"* defined by Webster, means the following: *"to remain firm under suffering or misfortune without yielding."* Christ suffered in the wilderness without yielding; you're going to have to do the same. You must remain firm in your commitment during the trying and uncomfortable moments during this challenge. There is no crown without a cross.

Daily, Christians face *"the lust of the flesh, and the lust of the eyes, and the pride of life,"* in some way, shape, or form; you are confronted with the world surrounding you and the will inside of you. These will become more heightened on your journey as your spiritual senses become more acutely aware as you begin to drink from your cup of self-denial. Such a phrase is scorned in today's society. The present culture that envelops us is an age where liberation is out of control, and *"if it feels good, just do it."* The moral lines in the sand have been erased, and nobody wants to take up their cross and deny themselves. This is where you come in. You're not like those around you. You're different. You have a higher calling. Let's look at Christ being tempted in the wilderness as He exposes the three inherent failures of man that were never seen before until His *unplugged* challenge.

Hebrews 4:12 says, *"forasmuch then as the children are partakers of flesh and blood, he also himself likewise took part of the same,"* validating the human nature of Christ. Within these scriptures, in Matthew, the battle of the Will of God vs. the will of man is revealed.

LUST OF THE FLESH: "TURN THESE STONES INTO BREAD"

And when the tempter came to him, he said, "If thou be
the Son of God, command that these stones be made bread."
— Matthew 4:3-4

Try to place yourself in Christ's shoes; He had just fasted for forty days, *"he was afterward an hungered."* While writing this portion of the book, a story shared with me years ago by one of my best friends, Scott, about his great grandfather during WWII comes to mind. I feel it's very fitting, and it accentuates the point.

Scott's grandfather was stationed in Europe, fighting with the ground forces. It was an early morning, and their platoon had just come upon a village that had been destroyed by the Germans, and it was void of any occupants. They were famished; they had not eaten in days and were stricken with hunger. They rummaged through all the cupboards in search of a morsel of food, hoping and praying they'd find anything of nutritional value to thwart the relentless hunger. But instead, all they found was stale molded bread. Disheartened and still hungry, the detachment continued with their military campaign advancing to their destination. All the while, Scott's great grandfather couldn't stop thinking about that bread. Nighttime had come, and his unit was retiring for the evening, except Scott's grandfather; the hunger was unbearable. They were hours away from the village, and with the Germans in the area, leaving could cost him his life. Nevertheless, the pangs of hunger overrode his judgment and drove him to do the unthinkable, and while his comrades were fast asleep, Scott's great grandfather headed back to the village.

Self-denial in the form of fasting will quickly bring to the surface, a will inside of you that you never knew existed. Hunger will drive a man to do the unthinkable. In the Bible, 2 Kings Chapter 6, Samaria has been besieged by Syria, and they are in a great famine. The torture of hunger had ravished Israel—a donkey's head was sold for eighty pieces of silver, and dove's dung sold for five pieces of silver. It had got so bad, women were boiling their children for dinner; hunger had driven them to cannibalism. Hunger will test your sanity, as in the case with Scott's Grandfather. Risking his life, he marched through the enemy's territory for a piece of bread.

Christ had to conquer His flesh's inner appetite to show us how and help save us from ours. *"Every man is tempted, when he is drawn away of his own lust, and enticed" (James 1:14).*

Scott's great grandfather returned to the village, hoping that, somehow, that moldy, stale bread would satisfy his hunger. When he found it, he closed his eyes and devoured it, and within seconds after consuming it, he began to vomit because of its moldiness. Sill hungry and somewhat sick, he headed back to where his fellow soldiers were sleeping. The hours passed, and dawn was nearing, and a horrifying image came into his view as he approached his company. At some point during the night, the Germans invaded their camp while the men were sleeping and killed every man in the platoon. Scott's great grandfather was the only one that survived. The story's moral is not to accentuate Scott's great grandfather's survival, but how hunger will drive a man to do the unthinkable and risk his life to satisfy it.

The tempter was the human desire to assuage the agony of severe hunger that the Lord felt as his body wrenched in pain from the denial of food. The ability to turn a stone into a piece of bread was the temptation He had to conquer. After all, He fed the children of Israel with manna for forty years in the wilderness. How easy would this be?

There will be times amid your suffering that the thoughts will come tempting you, to throw the towel in, and quit because you can. But that won't give you the freedom you desire. It will only be a temporary relief, and soon the regret of giving up will haunt you, and you'll still be *"plugged"* into your pain. *Philippians 4:13 says, "I can do all things through Christ which strengtheneth me."* You can do this.

LUST OF THE EYES: "ALL THESE KINGDOMS WILL I GIVE THEE"

And saith unto him, "All these things will I give thee, if thou wilt fall down and worship me."

— Matthew 4:9

I'm sure a lot of people have done this at some point in their life, myself included; you're driving down the expressway, and the billboard reads: *The Mega Millions next drawing is Wednesday for $340,000,000.00.* Instantly, the conversation starts in your head. You tell yourself all the nice things you would do for people if you had that much money and how it would help others. Then your mind shifts gears, and you begin to think of all the things you could buy for yourself. You imagine yourself on that boat you've always wanted, cruising through the open seas and without a care in the world. Next, you're standing in the foyer of your mansion, looking up at the stunning crystal chandler that hangs from the twenty-foot ceiling, or you're racing down the road in your favorite sports car--and the list goes on and on.

Large sums of money like *$340,000,000.00* (the current Mega Millions) and the sense of power it brings is a gateway to unleash appetites never before tempted. I believe the statistics state something like eighty percent of lottery winners, after a few short years, end up filing for bankruptcy. Many have died from substance abuse, and families have been destroyed. Such sad endings are the result of not being able to discipline their appetite.

Christ had that power, and He had to conquer the temptation to turn those stones into bread when he was crippled with hunger. Christ had to govern His every thought, and so must you and I. The Apostle Paul, in his writings to the Corinthian Church, implores them about fighting the temptations of human desire. *"There hath no temptation taken you but such as is common to man: but God is faithful, who will not suffer you to be tempted above that ye are able; but will with the temptation also make a way to escape"* *(1 Corinthians 10:13).* Jesus Christ is our way of escape, and as Christ, the Word of God is what we must use to conquer the things that try to draw us away.

Job 31:1 says, "I made a covenant with mine eyes." We have to be careful what we put in front of our eyes. There are many accounts in the Bible of those who allowed certain things they looked at to draw them away from God. Lots' wife was turned into a pillar of salt when she couldn't resist the temptation to look back when God told her not to (Genesis 19:26). Just after Israel had conquered the Promised Land, God had commanded them not to take anything in Jericho; it belonged to Him. However, by the name of Achan, one such a man couldn't resist the temptation when he saw the spoils of silver and gold. His decision to allow what he saw to circumvent the Word of God, in the end, cost him not only his life and his families but the lives of thirty-six men also (Joshua Chapter 7).

We have to make a covenant with our eyes because they are the doorway to a smorgasbord of desire. Christ rebuked the desire to yield to the temptation with the Word, and so must we if we're going to be victorious in this life.

THE PRIDE OF LIFE: "CAST THYSELF DOWN"

"If thou be the Son of God, cast thyself down: for it is written, He shall give his angels charge concerning thee: and in their hands, they shall bear thee up, lest at any time thou dash thy foot against a stone."

— Matthew 4:6

Here we see the Lord standing on the precipice of the unthinkable, suicide. The delusional state of hunger had prompted him to entertain the thought of jumping from his perch. Christ, knowing it would be impossible to die, yet had to fight the battle of pride in the throes of His discomfort. As we have seen in times of extremes suffering, man's human nature can become convoluted in its thinking. Christ knew as God it would be impossible to commit such an atrocity, yet the temptation to jump was the test of self-will. Just imagine if Christ had yielded and jumped, He never would have gone to the cross because His pride wouldn't have allowed it.

Pride is probably the hardest one out of man's three inherent failures to overcome. Pride is a chain; it's unapologetic, and one never wants to admit it's wrong. It boasts itself of all its accomplishments and is self-exalting. The King of Babylon, Nebuchadnezzar, is an excellent depiction of this. A compendium of his life can be found in King Solomon's writings, *"Pride goeth before destruction, and a haughty spirit before a fall"* (Proverbs 16:18). A lesson the King would never forget; read Chapter 4 of Daniel.

Warned by God in a dream, yet blinded by his aspirations of greatness, King Nebuchadnezzar failed to take heed to the stern warning, *"break off thy sins by righteousness, and thine iniquities by shewing mercy to the poor; if it may be a lengthening of thy tranquillity"* (Daniel 4:27). Like Nebuchadnezzar, we sometimes have to learn things the hard way because humbling ourselves is just too difficult.

> *At the end of twelve months he walked in the palace of the kingdom of Babylon.*
> *The king spoke, and said, "Is not this great Babylon, that I have built for the house of the kingdom by the might of my power, and for the honour of my majesty?"*
> *While the word was in the king's mouth, there fell a voice from heaven, saying, O king Nebuchadnezzar, to thee it is spoken; "The kingdom is departed from thee."*
> *"And they shall drive thee from men, and thy dwelling shall be with the beasts of the field: they shall make thee to*

eat grass as oxen, and seven times shall pass over thee, until thou know that the most High relet in the kingdom of men, and giveth it to whomsoever he will."

The same hour was the thing fulfilled upon Nebuchadnezzar: and he was driven from men, and did eat grass as oxen, and his body was wet with the dew of heaven, till his hairs were grown like eagles' feathers, and his nails like birds' claws.

— Daniel 4:29-33

God will go to great lengths to reach a man and try to stop him from self-destructing –like the dream He sent the King. Unfortunately, man is usually too blinded by his *"pride"* to take heed to the warning sent to him by God, like Nebuchadnezzar. Don't let *pride* stand in your way on this journey. King Nebuchadnezzar's pride temporarily cost him everything, including his sanity. Yet, God, who is rich in mercy, knew through the King's abasement that he would greatly humble himself and declare that the heavens rule. In the end, King Nebuchadnezzar was restored to his kingdom after his pride caused him to be deposed; Nebuchadnezzar's testimony:

"And at the end of the days I Nebuchadnezzar lifted up mine eyes unto heaven, and mine understanding returned unto me, and I blessed the most High, and I praised and honoured him that liveth for ever, whose dominion is an everlasting dominion, and his kingdom is from generation to generation:"

"And all the inhabitants of the earth are reputed as nothing: and he doeth according to his will in the army of heaven, and among the inhabitants of the earth: and none can stay his hand, or say unto him, What doest thou?"

"At the same time my reason returned unto me; and for the glory of my kingdom, mine honour and brightness returned unto me; and my counsellers and my lords sought unto me; and I was established in my kingdom, and excellent majesty was added unto me."

*"Now I Nebuchadnezzar praise and extol and honour the King of heaven, all whose works are truth, and his ways judgment: **and those that walk in pride** he is able to abase."*

— Daniel 4:34-37

Humility always wins, and in your journey, this lesson will play out. For Christ to have His Spiritual Kingdom, He had to first dethrone *"the pride of life."* He had to cast down His earthly crown *(the will of man)* to put on a Spiritual Crown *(the Will of God).* The Lord Jesus Christ was tempted just like you, yet He triumphed over humanity's three inherent failures in His 40-day challenge of *"unplugging"* from self. It was not easy, as you can see; there were trying moments for the Lord, and you will have yours.

The next 40-days will be a spiritual fast (if you opt to include a literal fast at any point during these next forty days, I encourage that it will be great for your inner man). You will be on a journey, and the Word of God is your weapon to combat those opposing thoughts like the Lord Jesus did. You will not be perfected at the end of forty days, but you will have conquered some things that have held you down for a long time. Let me say this also, this is not the end; it's really just the beginning. You will realize, as I did, there just are somethings that will be impossible to disconnect from because they are attached to other people. People who are not willing to let go or incapable of putting certain things behind them. You must move on and not let others detour you from meeting your objective of being *unplugged!*

Furthermore, at the end of this 40-day challenge, it will be the beginning of a new you. Personally, God has spoken to me more vividly, clearly, and daily during the 40-day challenge than He has before. Why, you might ask? Because I'm not "plugged" into the white noise that surrounds me. As a result, God's voice has become clearer.

You must cognitively censor what goes in your thoughts. It is a direct correlation to what feeds your emotions. You will better understand the enemy within when the Word of God becomes your psychological filter. It's one thing to quote the Bible; it's another thing to live and breathe it. Matthew 6:24 states, *"No man can serve two masters."* It's either God's Will or your will. There is no in-between; it's all or nothing.

"For we have not an high priest which cannot be touched with the feeling of our infirmities; but was in all points tempted like as we are, yet without sin" (Hebrews 4:15). Christ went through what you're about to; He has felt the infirmities of being tempted like you will. He had to so that He could be relatable to your pain.

UNPLUGGED FOR 40 DAYS, AND 40 NIGHTS

And the glory of the LORD abode upon mount Sinai, and the cloud covered it six days: and the seventh day he called unto Moses out of the midst of the cloud. And the sight of the glory of the LORD was like devouring fire on the top of the mount in the eyes of the children of Israel. And Moses went into the midst of the cloud, and gat him up into the mount: and Moses was in the mount forty days and forty nights And he gave unto Moses, when he had made an end of communing with him upon mount Sinai, two tables of testimony, tables of stone, written with the finger of God.

– Exodus 24:16-18, Exodus 31:18

This is the beginning of the Bible, as we know it, in written form. Up until this point in Israel's history, it was just folklore; stories were handed down from generation to generation. It didn't take forty days for God to write the Ten Commandments and the Law. It took 40-days for Moses to *unplug,* from himself, to be in the place to receive what God not only had for him but for the nation of Israel. Even though this journey is about you, others will reap and benefit from it. Is there some type of psychological transformation that occurs after 40-days? Medically speaking, I don't know? But, I know through the scripture that there is a Spiritual transformation that will manifest itself.

Mountain climbing is not easy, and along the way, you may slip and fall, but you've got to get back up and keep going. I'm sure Moses' trek up the mountain wasn't paved and without an incline. There was blood, sweat, and tears shed in the process of getting to the place where God told Moses to meet Him. Get ready to shed some blood, sweat, and tears on your way to receive the best God has for you, at the top of the mountain, where He's waiting.

40-days are inescapable, whether you decide to take the challenge or not. So, why not take advantage of the opportunity at hand, and accept the challenge. In chapter twelve, I shared a sample of the journal. I hope you will embrace the challenge and experience what 40-days in a spiritual mountain with God can do for you.

CHAPTER 12

A ROAD MAP FOR YOUR SUCCESSFUL JOURNEY

"This book of the law shall not depart out of thy mouth; but thou shalt meditate therein day and night, that thou mayest observe to do according to all that is written therein: for then thou shalt make thy way prosperous, and then thou shalt have good success." "Have not I commanded thee? Be strong and of a good courage; be not afraid, neither be thou dismayed: for the LORD thy God is with thee whithersoever thou goest."

– Joshua 1:8-9

Herein lies the secret of Joshua being a victorious leader and Israel a winning nation. Herein lies the secret to you being a victorious Christian and a winning leader. *Unplugging* your mind from the fray of life and *plugging* it into the Word of God. Romans 12:2 states exactly what this book is about. *"Be not conformed to this world: but be ye transformed by the renewing of your mind."* *Unplugging* is the renewing of your mind, soul, and spirit.

The Book Of The Law Shall Not Depart Of Your Mouth.

You have to speak the Word when doubt and any other contrary thing want to come forth. Death and life are in the power of the tongue. Speak your victory, not your defeat!

You Must Meditate On The Book Day And Night.

God commanded Joshua to meditate on His Word, day and night because anything else could sway his faith in God's possibilities for Israel. The same applies to you. You must focus on putting God's Word at the forefront of your thoughts so doubts do not prevail.

A Prosperous Way And Good Success.

It's not the Lord's Will for His people to struggle and be miserable. It's not a good witness to the world for you to walk around looking down in the dumps. God's people should always have a smile on their faces and an attitude of gratitude. King David penned one of my favorite scriptures in Psalms 34:1: *"I will bless the LORD at all times: his praise shall continually be in my mouth."* "At all times" means not only when things are good but also when things go wrong. David's life encompassed both ends of the spectrum, grief and joy, and yet, he always had praise for God, and so should we.

When the Lord appeared to Moses at the burning bush, He said, *"I have surely seen the affliction of my people which are in Egypt, and have heard their cry by reason of their taskmasters; for I know their sorrows; And I am come down to deliver them out of the hand of the Egyptians, and to bring them up out of that land unto a good land and a large, unto a land flowing with milk and honey" (Exodus 3:7-8).* God has seen your affliction and heard your cry and wants to help you *unplug* from your pain and bring you into a land that flows with milk and honey.

"A land that flows with milk and honey" is a land of prosperity. Something that *"flows"* is in perpetual motion; that source continuously pushes out its substance, is God's favor in our life. *"Milk and honey"* are indicative of both spiritual and natural prosperity. According to these scriptures, God wants a prosperous way for His people, and He wants Good Success for them. Good Success will only come from obedience to His Word.

HAVE I NOT COMMANDED THEE, BE STRONG AND OF GOOD COURAGE BE NOT AFRAID

Fear of failure is a ploy of your inherent nature, trying to use your past failures against you. This mind will convince you not to believe what God says. This is not what God commanded Joshua, and it's not what He commanded you. God said, *"Have not I command thee"?* God commands you to do certain things He knows will cause you to face your fears of failure, and this is where He gets all the glory. During this journey, you will have to confront and face your fears and unbelief, but God commands you. It's all part of bringing you into the promises of His Word, into the "land that flows with milk and honey." Be strong, and of good courage, and be NOT afraid!

FOR THE LORD THY GOD IS WITH THEE

Jesus said unto the disciples, ***"lo I am with you always, even unto the end of the world."*** *(Matthew 28:20)* The Lord is with you until the end!

I want to summarize with the five F's of what this book is about, ***"Faith, Forgiven, Forgive, Freedom, And Forward."*** It takes faith to believe you've been forgiven. Because you've been forgiven, you can forgive. Because you can forgive, you now have freedom. Freedom allows you to move forward on a road map for a successful life; this is the secret of being *"unplugged"!*

A roadmap indeed will be the key to a successful journey. Please look at the templet on the next page of the journal. It will be a strong support for the journey and a critical key to your good success and a prosperous way.

THE END

Journal Sample:

The signs will not only act as a natural guide but also spiritual. This is the spiritual interstate 40. Along this interstate, there will be road signs giving directions, warnings, and other information. The 12th chapter title says, "A Road Map For a Successful Journey," and that's exactly what this journal will be. We know the Lord was an avid proponent of symbology, and we're going to do the same. We'll be using the things you cross daily in the path of life or in your travels, which will act as a reminder of what this journey is about.

"Straight paths make for your feet" (Hebrews 12:13). There is no U-turn, only a straight path where your victory will be waiting for you at the finish line.

Starting Date: _____

Signature: _____

    This is a contract with yourself. You are signing a deal to victory over all the things you've been *plugged* into.

THE THINGS I WILL BE "UNPLUGGING" FROM:

_____

_____

_____

_____

MY ATTITUDE ABOUT TAKING THE "UNPLUGGED" CHALLENGE:

_____

_____

_____

_____

WHAT AM I UNPLUGGING FROM?

_____

_____

_____

_____

WHY AM I UNPLUGGING?

_____

_____

_____

_____

HOW AM I UNPLUGGING?

_____

_____

_____

_____

OTHER NOTES:

_____

_____

_____

_____

Day 1.

Congratulations! Today is the day your journey begins. You've just crossed the intersection, and there is no turning back. This is a one-way road. For some, this journey started a long time ago in your mind and heart, when you decided that you wanted a change in your walk with the Lord. I commend you because many people won't accept what you have (the Unplugged challenge), and they will never get to experience the freedom you will from this!

"Remember, face each day with the expectation of achieving good rather than the dread of falling short."

Today's Unplugging Goals:

_____

_____

_____

How Do You Feel About You "Unplugging" These Things?

_____

_____

_____

Write A Scripture That Will Help You Focus On Meeting Your Objective:

_____

_____

_____

Day 7.

"Nay, in all these things we are more than conquerors through him that loved us."

— Romans 8:37

Congratulations, you've made it. You've got one week in the books on building a better you! You are now one week into your journey. On any road trips you'll take, you'll see this sign along the way. A rest area is critical for your success; no one can travel non-stop without taking a break; you'll get burned out. Pull over and get refreshed. I didn't say stop, simply pull over and rest. Today you decide how it's going to go. Below I modified the comment columns and added a section. Be honest and fill in the blanks!

How is your progress on meeting your objective?

_____

_____

_____

How do you feel about what you are unplugging from?

_____

_____

_____

In your spirit, are you questioning why you're doing this? If so, write it down?

_____

_____

_____

Write a scripture that will help you focus on meeting your objective.

_____

_____

_____

Day 20.

"Well done is better than well said…an ounce of example is better than a pound of advice."

You've reached the peak of the mountain today; you're at the half waypoint. Not only are you doing well, but your life has also become an example to others, and more importantly, to yourself.

How is your progress on meeting your objective?

_____

_____

_____

How do you feel about what you are unplugging from?

_____

_____

_____

_____

In your spirit, are you questioning why you're doing this? If so, write it down.

_____

_____

_____

Write a scripture that will help you focus on meeting your objective.

_____

_____

_____

Day 40.

As you can see, this is going to be fun, exciting, and emotional. I encourage you to purchase the journal and get the best of what God's got in store for your life.

ABOUT THE AUTHOR

Thomas L. Teal Jr. was born and raised in Michigan, attended high school in Imlay City, and now lives in Shelby Township, a northern suburb of Detroit, with his wife, Laura. He owns and runs a construction business.

From a young age, Thomas became enthused with writing, and he began writing short stories, poems, and songs. This passion remained within him throughout his life.

Encouraged by his wife, Thomas wrote his first book, **Unplugged**. In it, the reader is taken on a journey of self-scrutiny, discovery, and healing based on faith in God.

Thomas enjoys keeping fit, fishing, riding his bike, and writing in his free time. He has a strong foundation in the Apostolic faith, teaches in-home bible studies, and devotes some of his time to treatment centers, helping those struggling with addiction.

Thomas aspires to eventually become a full-time writer, reaching out to others and helping and inspiring them in their walk with the Lord and in life. His favorite quote is *"The Secret of Living is Giving…"* - Pastor W.J. Davidson

You can contact or follow Thomas L. Teal Jr. at:
Twitter: **@thomaslteal**
Instagram: **thomaslteal**
Facebook: **Thomas Teal**
Email: **thomaslteal@gmail.com**

Made in the USA
Monee, IL
07 June 2021